RAINBOW PEOPLE

RAINBOW PEOPLE

Material for use in holiday clubs with children of 5-12 years
— theory, biblical teaching and practical ideas

by

Marian Carter

Acknowledgements

My thanks go to Diana Drayson, Jean Humphrey and Leslie Francis who gave of their time and energy to encourage and advise.

Dedication

I would like to dedicate this book to the children from whom I have learnt so much.

Cover Illustration: Sarah West
Illustrations: Wendy Carolan
Cynthia Dummet

Published by:
National Christian Education Council
Robert Denholm House
Nutfield
Redhill RH1 4HW

British Library Cataloguing-in-Publication Data:
Carter, Marian
 Rainbow People
 I. Title
 259
 ISBN 0-7197- 0790-0

First published 1992
© Marian Carter 1992

Typesetting by One & A Half Graphics, Redhill, Surrey.
Printed in Great Britain by BPCC-AUP Aberdeen Ltd.

CONTENTS

Many churches use the school holidays to run short, intensive holiday clubs for children. These clubs may be for members of their existing organisations, the children of church members or children living in the neighbourhood who have no church connection. Some clubs invite children from each of these groups. But what is a holiday club and what is its purpose?

A holiday club is a time of fun and activities through which children and adults come to learn more about God and the good news of Jesus while working and playing together. It is part of the ongoing mission and educational programme of the church's work with children. It is founded on three principles:

☐ *Theological* – the Christian nurture of children.

☐ *Psychological* – the development of positive attitudes.

☐ *Educational* – the use of a proven method of learning.

The Theological Principle

Christian learning develops within a community of faith - the church. In a holiday club the adult helpers are the representatives of a faith community. They teach children through a variety of methods including stories, games and activities. But more importantly they introduce children to faith through experiences of worship and the example of their own lives. It is through such encounters that children may recognise God at work in their own lives and respond to God's call. The theological principle underlying this experience is that of *Christian nurture*.

Christian nurture concerns the growth and development of an individual as a member of a Christian community. It is more than learning facts about the faith, rather it is an introduction to the way of life that makes Christian people different from those who are not Christian. Worship is a distinctive characteristic of Christians. Within worship the community offers its own everyday life and experience and sets it alongside the stories of God's people as told in the Scriptures. Reflection on the interaction of life experience and the scripture experience of God's people leads to a greater understanding of where God is at work in our lives, and of God's will and purposes for each of us.

The Psychological Principle

A holiday club is, for some children, their first experience of the church. It is important that this encounter is warm and positive. For the children of members, and those belonging to a church organisation, a holiday club may be an occasion when faith takes on a new meaning in their lives or a time when faith deepens. For all the children the experience needs to be one in which the church, both building and people, becomes a place where they want to be. They know that here they, and their contribution, will be valued. It will be a time when barriers between children and church are broken down. Underlying this thinking are certain psychological principles concerned with *attitude formation*.

The ages of 7-11 years are important for forming attitudes. Researchers tell us these persist into, and influence, adult life. As Christians we believe it is important for children that their attitudes towards the church and Christian faith are positive ones. Positive attitudes are fostered when children feel they are respected for themselves, that their interests and needs are understood, and that these are significant to the adults around them.

The Educational Principle

For it to be effective, children need to be involved in their own learning. They learn by doing things and enjoying what they do. Their experience becomes the springboard for reflection and further learning.

One method of learning from experience is through projects. These identify a theme and encourage the children to explore it from many angles, through fact finding, discovery and the use of the imagination. Later, the findings can be displayed on charts and posters, and expressed through dance, art, music and poetry. The educational principle of learning through experience has been tried and tested through its use in our Primary Schools.

Holiday clubs can provide children with an enjoyable experience of a faith community, so that they will at some point ask what it means to be part of that community with its distinctive beliefs and way of life.

Rainbow People is designed so that children can enjoy a Bible story together, and relate it to their own concrete experience, so that they may understand more of God and grow in faith.

About the Material

Rainbow People has twin foci:

> **The biblical story.**
> **The experience of the child.**

The biblical tradition is based on the Genesis story of Noah's Flood. At one level the story is simple. It tells of a great flood which destroys the earth and everything living except Noah, his family and a pair of each animal species. Following the flood, life begins again with the rainbow as a sign of God's promise that the world would never again be destroyed by a flood. Underlying the story are important statements about the nature of God and God's relationship to creation. The story teaches that:

- God weeps over sinful creation.
- God decides to wipe out sin.
- God chooses to flood the earth.
- God is love and chooses not to make this a final end.

- So God chooses Noah.

- God provides the ark to save Noah.

- Noah chooses to cooperate with God.

- Noah builds the ark.

- Noah is called to leave the ark and begin life again.

- God chooses a binding relationship between God and Noah.

- God's promise is seen in the rainbow.

- All is God's initiative and God's grace.

The Bible's flood story explores powerful human experiences of sin, judgment, renewal and re-creation. God's relationship with Noah is a model of God's dealings with each of us, holding out new life and promise when we are overwhelmed by our own sinfulness. The story of Noah looks forward to the saving grace which is shown fully in Jesus.

At first the statements listed above may seem remote from the experiences of the children. The children know the power of their own emotions of anger and jealousy which are so strong they seem overwhelming. They are aware that somehow the world around them is marred and not as it was intended. Children know about wanting to make a clean start and begin again, as when they spoil a page in a school exercise book and long to turn over to a fresh, clean page. They want to know that their world is reliable and it will continue, and that promises are kept. Thus the children's experiences reflect and interrelate with the biblical tradition.

Rainbow People selects five concrete images from the Noah story - Noah, The Ark, Water, The Dove, and The Rainbow. The story is told as a serial with five parts. The biblical images are set alongside parallels in the experiences of the children. The children are given opportunities to reflect and discover how the Bible speaks to them and make sense of their experiences.

Day 1 - Noah

Noah is an ordinary person who is chosen by God. God asks him to build an ark. Noah trusts God, although he understands little of what is to happen. As Noah trusts, so God is able to use him. Noah is everyone - you and me. God calls us and as we trust God, we are able to work with God to help make a better world.

Day 2 - The Ark

God calls for the building of an ark. The ark has traditionally been understood as a symbol of sanctuary from the confusion and evil of the world, but the ark also weathers the storm and enters the new world. Children create their own sanctuaries and call them 'dens'. We look at God's provision of safe places for us.

Day 3 – Water

The flood waters destroy, purify and renew life. Water is a powerful religious symbol of both life and death. It is used in baptism as the symbol of putting away an old life and beginning a new one. Children use water everyday. Here we explore the symbol of water as it cleanses and renews.

Day 4 - The Dove

The dove and the olive branch it carries are both symbols of peace. After the flood waters and the destruction of sin and evil comes peace and new life. Children face conflict situations and know their need for renewed relationships and the restoring of peace. We explore how peace is restored after conflicts and discover God's gift of peace.

Day 5 - The Rainbow

The rainbow is the sign of God's ongoing promise to creation that it will never again be destroyed. Children need stability in their lives; they need to know that God keeps promises.

This material has been written for use with children aged between five and twelve. If needed, you could extend it to include pre-schoolers and those in their early teens. Suggestions are provided for five half day sessions with further optional activities to create material for a whole week. This allows flexibility: use the material for five half days or five whole days.

Each unit contains three parts:

Leader's Preparation

Teaching material

Resources

LEADER'S PREPARATION

This section is designed to be used by the adults taking part in the club, working as a group. You will need to prepare well in advance of the holiday club, sharing ideas as a group. It is surprising the hidden talents which are discovered in individuals when they work together! It is useful to appoint a team leader to guide the use of the material in the group. This section is not intended for use with the children.

Understanding the Bible

The Bible story presents particular insights about God, and God's relationship with us. The Noah story has been chosen as the theme of this material because of what it teaches about God's initiative in forgiveness and re-creation, which are examples of God's saving work of grace. It is God who is at the centre of the story. God calls Noah to respond and works with Noah. The biblical insights need to be explored in detail in order to understand the passage.

Background material

As adults, we need to understand the concepts underlying the theme in our own experience before preparing to work with the children. This section explores the concepts in the Bible and in everyday life, to help the leader begin to make his or her own connections.

Image

Each day one image from the Bible passage is chosen. The exploring of the child's experience and the practical projects are created around this image.

Objectives

Each session is built around four objectives: simple statements of what it is intended the children will learn in the session. Keep them in mind at all times in order that your learning time together is as worthwhile as possible. At the end of each session, use these objectives to assess the effectiveness of your teaching: did the children learn what you wished them to?

Teaching Material

This section makes practical suggestions for working with the children. Several alternatives have been given so that you can choose those which best meet your needs. But don't stop there! Use your creative originality! Be prepared to adapt these suggestions, or to think of new ones, that fit your own situation.

Rainbow Time 1

The beginning of each session is a time for children of all ages to meet together to worship. It is a time for singing, prayer and listening to the Bible story. It is the time when the day's image is introduced using one of three suggested options.

Group activities

The main activities of the club are undertaken in smaller groups. It is helpful if these groups are age related. The ideal child to adult ratio is about 6-8 children per adult. As children's needs, interests and abilities vary according to their ages, different suggestions are given for 5-7 year olds and for 8-12 year olds.

Each day follows the same pattern as explained below:

Sharing

Begin the session with the children sharing some of their own experiences, and then see how these have parallels with the story in the Bible. Children are self-centred and need to use concrete personal experiences as a springboard to understand the feelings of other people.

Exploring the Bible

Guidelines are given for the leader to help them share the Bible story in their own words. An example of how to tell the story is given in each day's **Resources** section.

Talking

This section makes connections between the sections **Sharing** and **Exploring the Bible**; the child's experience and the experiences of the people of God in the Scriptures.

Creating

A choice of activities is included, requiring different amounts of time and varying levels of skill. Select your activity according to your resources of space, time and personnel. Some suggested activities are described in each day's **Resources** section; others can be found in the appendix at the back of the book.

Rainbow Time 2

The morning session ends with a short period when the whole club can come together to share what they have discovered and made.

Resources

This section contains suggestions to help you with your preparation for each session:

- A play which can be used as an introduction during **Rainbow Time**. It is fun if prepared by the adult helpers. No special acting ability is needed and scripts can be discreetly used. Humour is slap-stick, encouraging the children to join in.

- Story: the day's section of the flood story, to help the leader tell the story in their own words. The story could also be used in **Rainbow Time** as the Bible reading.

- Appropriate songs from books which may be familiar to the children:
  - *Alleluya!* (A & C Black Ltd)
  - *Someone's Singing Lord* (A & C Black Ltd)
  - *Come and Praise* (BBC Enterprises)
  - *The Oxford Assembly Book* (Oxford University Press)

- A game which reflects the day's theme and helps reinforce the learning process.

- *Creative Resources* Diagrams and instructions for practical activities.

Suggestions for the afternoon sessions follow those for the morning. These sessions will give the children an opportunity to explore the theme creatively and imaginatively.

Morning

10.00-10.15	Registration of children

10.15-10.30   **Rainbow Time 1** (everyone)
Theme Song 'The Rainbow Song'
Singing and praying
Scripture reading
Introduction to the theme for the day
Birthdays and Notices

10.30-12.30   **Activities in age groups**
Sharing
Exploring the Bible
Drink and biscuit
   (approximately 11.15 – use a natural break)
Creating
Talking

12.30-12.45   **Rainbow Time 2** (everyone)
Sharing together the morning activities

12.45-13.15   Picnic lunch

Afternoon   (Further details are given on page 66)

13.15-13.30   Registration and list of afternoon groups

13.30-15.30   **Choice of activities** (mixed age groups)
for example:
Music workshop
Making musical instruments
Banner making

Three afternoons   Cooking
Drama workshop
Outdoor sports
Indoor sports
Painting
Craft Workshop

Fourth afternoon   Sports/Games afternoon

Fifth afternoon   Outing related to the theme for example; a water sport: ice rink, swimming pool, boating, seaside; old working water mill, reservoir, water purifying works, a bird sanctuary, safari park etc.

15.30-16.00   **Rainbow Time** (everyone)
Theme song
Sharing
Notices
Dismissal

Below are some practical hints about the preparations necessary to run a successful holiday club.

1. Personnel

Many skills are needed to run a club. People should not feel excluded because they 'can't teach'. The adults needed include:

- Organiser — to call meetings, plan, oversee, a 'figure head'.

- Secretary — to be responsible for secretarial work before the club; during the club to keep the central register.

- Leaders — to prepare the activities for the children.

- Musicians — to prepare the songs for the daily worship time.

- Helpers — to prepare the drinks for the daily break time. To take responsibility for resources – *for example:* the preparation of paints, brushes, scissors and paper. Equip each group and collect returned equipment.

- First Aid — a trained person with a well stocked first aid box is essential.

This list is not exhaustive, other tasks can be added as necessary. The above list means that the work is shared. Some parents may welcome an opportunity to be involved. Members of the church not normally involved in children's work can be invited to participate.

2. Meetings

You will need to meet regularly before your club begins in order to be prepared. First, decide the dates your club will run, then work back from this allowing several sessions for:

- practical preparation,

- content preparation.

You will find that a first session at least three months before your club begins will be most helpful. It is important that everyone knows their tasks, and that each person is adequately prepared and supported by the other adult helpers and the prayers of the whole church.

3. Advertising

The number of children you can accept for your club will depend on the premises available and the number of volunteer helpers. It is important to have a good ratio of adults to children, even if this means refusing some children. Central to the learning of the holiday club is the relationships built during the sessions.

Decide the numbers you can reasonably accommodate.

You can advertise:

- through the local free press,
- by handing out notices through local schools, with the permission of the head teacher,
- through enthusiastic children and adults telling their friends.

Your application forms should include a reply slip to be returned by a specific date - at least a month before the club commences. This should include details such as:

- name of child,
- age of child,
- address and phone number,
- signature of parent or guardian.

An example of a reply-slip appears in the Appendix of this book; this can be adapted or photocopied as required.

If you are charging for the club, include details of the charge. Remember that we often value a thing more if we have to pay something towards it! The charge should cover the cost of materials and refreshments.

4. Prayer partners

Write the names of all the children who will be joining the club on a sheet of paper. Invite members of the congregation to take a sheet and pray for the children and the adult helpers.

5. Brochure

When you know the names of group leaders and helpers, the names of the children and their activity groups, the times of the club and details of any visits, prepare a brochure for each participant with these details. Include a tear-off return slip for parents to sign with details such as:

- any medical needs of the child,
- phone number of a parent or guardian in case of an emergency.

An example return slip appears in the Appendix of this book; this can be adapted or photocopied as required.

The brochure could be delivered to each home by the group leader. This is an opportunity for the leader to introduce themselves to the parents or guardians and answer any questions.

6. Leaders' preparation

It is useful for the leaders to meet together at least twice to work through the material carefully and prayerfully.

Preparation will include:

- choosing approach and activities,

- making lists of the resources needed,

- cutting out models,

- creating fun worksheets for odd moments,

- making a name badge for each child for the first day,

- song sheets.

7. Decorate the church or hall

Decorate the room(s) being used for the club so that the atmosphere is welcoming, and exciting to the children.

Display a permanent symbol such as the rainbow. You might consider having an 'entrance' with a password and passes! Make sure you have spare passes for those that get mislaid. If the child's name is on the pass it is useful for registering the children. Hand the pass to the group leader at the beginning of the day. It is returned by the leader at the end of the day for use the following day. The entrance could be the gang plank into the ark!

At the end of the afternoon, registration is simplified through a fun activity, such as inventing a game around returning the passes.

An example of a club pass appears in the Appendix of this book; this can be adapted or photocopied as required.

8. Begin Collecting

At least a month before the event advertise your needs and start collecting, for example:

- old newspapers,

- sheets,

- yogurt pots, egg boxes, cereal boxes,

- fabric oddments for banners,

- oddments of emulsion paint,

- bin bags to slit and use for aprons,

- sheets of polythene to protect floors while painting.

Approach your Local Authority Play Council who may provide a grant, give materials and loan equipment.

Borrow a collection of source books from the library for model making and stories of the rainbow from other cultures. (See Friday - **The Rainbow**)

Keep your eyes and ears open. It is amazing what materials you can find. Manufacturers are often willing to give away useful off-cuts if they know the material will be used by children.

9. Take-homes

It is useful to have a folder for each child, in which they can store their own work. It can be taken home at the end of the week as a record of achievement, and in addition, shared with parents.

10. Follow-on

Finally, think about how the activities of the club can be shared with the wider church as a climax to the week.

One idea is a *Sunday Celebration Festival of Worship*. Some of the songs can be introduced to the congregation. Have a performance of *Captain Noah and his Floating Zoo* from the Music Workshop. Display children's work. This shows both children and parents that you value the children and what they have achieved. Follow the worship by a picnic lunch for children and parents.

Use the interest and enthusiasm you generate. Prepare flyers of the regular organisations for children in your church. Give them out as children leave. Invite those not yet involved to join. Encourage the children to become part of the on-going membership of the church.

Now to work! Holiday clubs are fun - even the preparation can be enjoyable as adults who may not know one another very well begin to work together.

GENESIS 6.5-14

LEADER'S PREPARATION
Understanding the Bible

The fact that we know little about Noah is deliberate, for the 'hero' of the story is not Noah but God. Noah becomes important because he responds to God's call by building the ark. It is through Noah that God is able to save a remnant to be the beginning of a new creation.

Looking at creation, God declared it 'very good' but now it had gone wrong. Everywhere there was violence and evil, the result of human selfishness and sin. Genesis describes God's grief and sorrow and the decision to destroy the earth by flood and begin again. God judges human sin; God, however, is loving and love cannot destroy what it has made. Then God sees Noah and chooses him to be the representative of the human race to begin creation anew after the flood. God instructs Noah on the building of an ark in which he and his family will be saved.

Genesis emphasizes that God had chosen Noah before the judgement of the flood so that God's work of salvation could continue. Part of the story suggests that Noah builds the ark without knowing its purpose; it is only as Noah enters the ark that he learns of God's plan to destroy the earth. Noah is described as 'righteous' and 'blameless': the Hebrew word which is used means 'pleasing to God' – Noah was trustworthy and obedient.

Background material

The story of Noah is a model of God's relationship with each one of us. We know little of Noah before the flood story except his name and those of his three sons. The later story of his drunkeness and exposure (*Genesis 9.21*) suggests that he was no plaster saint, yet God used him. Noah was chosen by God to take humanity from the old age into the new. Noah had a choice. He chose to trust God. In the *Letter to the Hebrews* he is used as an example of a man of great faith. Noah worked in cooperation with God to enable a world spoilt by sin to become the kind of world that God intended.

Each of us recognises within ourselves the mixture of good and bad. In religious terms, we are created in the image and likeness of God, but we fail to fulfill this potential. Yet God knows us each one, accepts us and calls us, as we are. Children need help to know that they are loved with all their strengths and weaknesses. God loves them as they are. Like Noah, they can choose to respond to God's call.

Image: Noah

Objectives

☐ to relate the story of God's choice of Noah,

☐ to show how God uses Noah – and us when we trust him,

☐ to help each child to realise their uniqueness,

☐ to help the children discover they are loved and called by God.

TEACHING MATERIAL

Rainbow Time 1

Display the Rainbow symbol of your holiday club.
Theme song (page 70) and other songs (see today's **Resources**).
Introduce the image to the whole group in one of the following ways:

● The play (see today's **Resources**),

● A sheet of paper (large enough for all to see) with six personal questions written on it; for example –

— How tall are you?
— How much do you weigh?
— Where were you born?
— Where do you live now?
— Do you have any brothers and sisters? How many?

You will need to have prepared these questions earlier, and you should provide a tape measure and scales to check the children's information. Ask a volunteer to come to the front where everyone can see and hear, and write down the volunteer's answer to each question. Now repeat the question to the whole group, inviting anyone with an answer the same as the volunteer's to raise a hand. Finally, ask if there is anyone with *six* answers the same as the volunteer's. It is unlikely; ask why. Draw out from the children the recognition that we are each unique.

● Have prepared a picture of Noah made by drawing an outline with candle wax on a large sheet of paper. This will be invisible. Provide a pot of black paint and a brush. Ask the children what they know about Noah. Any child offering correct information is invited to help 'discover' Noah by painting over part of the picture. The wax resists the paint and gradually Noah is revealed.

Group Activities 5-7 year olds

Sharing

Invite the children to look at someone else's face. Encourage close observation. Discuss the similarities and differences between them.

- some are boys, some girls,
- the colour of eyes, hair and skin differs,
- each has eyes and ears,
- each is different,
- each is unique and loved by God.

Exploring the Bible Genesis 6.5-14

Tell the story of Noah's family, and how he was chosen by God. Use the suggestions in **Resources** or enlarge on the points below. You could tell the story with a refrain spoken by the children – for example: *God chose Noah.*

- God created a good world,
- the world was spoilt by people's selfishness,
- God decided to destroy the world and begin again,
- God loved all God had made,
- God chose Noah to build an ark,
- Noah had three sons Shem, Ham and Japheth,
- God saved Noah and his family in the ark,
- God chose Noah to help build the new world.

Talking

Explore with the children any actions they are proud of, or which make them feel ashamed. Help them to discover that they are loved for themselves. They are loved and called by God, just as Noah was.

Creating

Choose one or more of the following options:

- make a book with the title *I'm special,*
- look in a mirror and draw a self portrait. Use circles of card for the faces and strands of wool for hair. (The faces could be used later as crew for the ark),
- create pictures of Noah and his family by drawing round a child lying on the floor. Colour the pictures, or outline using pieces of sticky paper or lengths of fabric. Decorate with twists of coloured tissue paper,
- make papier mâché hand puppets of Noah and his family to use in your own play of the story (see today's **Creative Resources**),
- draw or paint a picture of Noah and his family.

Group Activities 8-12 year olds

Sharing

Provide *mirrors* so the children can draw self-portraits. Use these to explore differences and similarities among the group, *for example:*

- differences in colouring,
- similarities in colouring,
- the uniqueness of each individual.

Exploring the Bible

Use the biblical material for 5-7 year olds adding the following:

- that little is known about Noah. God is the 'hero' of the story,
- that Noah was chosen as a representative human,
- that he was an ordinary person,
- include the incident after the flood, when Noah got drunk,
- discuss how Noah trusted God, so enabling God to use him.

Talking

Ask the children in what ways *they* are like Noah. Think of the mixture of good and bad that we all are. Talk about any occasions when the children have been choosen to represent others, for example: thanking a school visitor or participating in a school team in competition with another school.

Creating

Choose one or more of the following options:

- Make your own passport.
- Make life size models of Noah and his family (See today's **Creative Resources**).
- In pairs, begin work on a book for the programme 'Noah – *This is your Life.'* Add to it during the week.
- Imagine you are Noah and write a poem about why God chose you.
- Make a collage of pictures or words showing the world as God intended it to be – for example: cooperation between humans, or care of the environment.

Rainbow Time 2

Use this time together to share what each group has made and discovered.

RESOURCES

These useful resources will help you in your planning. Select those which are most helpful in your particular situation.

Play

This play can be used in **Rainbow Time 1** to introduce your theme:

The One and Only Captain Noah

Characters:	Noah
	Mrs Noah
	Shem, Ham and Japheth (their sons)
	Three wives

Noah enters the room and discovers the audience.

NOAH

Hello! Are you visitors? I'm Noah. Well, aren't you going to say hello? *(He holds a card up which says Hello Noah! He waves it around)* I'm an ordinary fellow. I try to do the right thing but sometimes I get out of bed the wrong side. I lose my temper and kick the cat. I like a little drink – sometimes I drink too much and then ... *(He mimicks being drunk and falls around the room finally doing a somersault. He sits as if telling a story)* Life went along; getting up – working – eating – sleeping – going to bed. Getting up – working – eating – sleeping – going to bed ...Then one day God said I was needed. Me – Noah!

Suddenly the story is interrupted by the entrance of the family.

SHEM

Hello, Dad! *(Turns to children)* I'm Shem.

HAM

Hello, Dad! *(He too turns to the children)* I'm Ham.

JAPHETH

Hello, Dad! *(To the children)* I'm the last, I'm Japheth.

NOAH

My three sons ... but where are the ladies?

Mrs Noah enters followed by the three wives.

MRS NOAH

We're working while you chat! *(She chases Noah around with her broom)* What's going on, husband?

WIVES

Yes – what's going on?

NOAH

(Pointing to the audience) I'm telling these children the story about God choosing me. You can listen. *(They all sit round Noah and listen)* At the beginning of time everyone lived happily together. That's how God made it, and 'it was good'. Then people got selfish. One person got jealous of another and picked a quarrel *(Sons get up and have a mock punch up)* No – not you! Don't you start! *(To the children)* See what I mean? Because of all the violence God decided to flood the earth and destroy everthing, then to start again.

MRS NOAH	You mean drown everyone? But God *made* everyone! Didn't God love them?
NOAH	Yes! God loved them – but God didn't love what they were doing. God hated all the evil. Then God thought of a plan – that's where I came in.
HAM	*You?*
NOAH	Yes, God chose to save *me* from the flood to help build a new world.
HAM	What about us?
NOAH	Well, you too. I suppose because you're family ...
JAPHETH	You *chosen!* Why were *you* chosen?
NOAH	Well ... *(Struts up and down proudly)*
SETH	Well? It wasn't your good looks!
HAM	Nor your trendy clothes ...
JAPHETH	I bet it was because you have three handsome sons!
WIVES	No – it was your pretty daughters-in-law.
MRS NOAH	*I* think you were chosen because of your capable wife.
MALES	Oh, no you weren't! *(Encourage children to join in)*
FEMALES	Oh, yes you were! *(Encourage children to join in)*
NOAH	You're all wrong! God chose me because ...
MRS NOAH	Well, why? God must have had a reason.
NOAH	For no reason except that God is God. And God is my friend.
MRS NOAH	See! I told you so – you are special. That's why you were chosen.
HAM	You're unique.
JAPHETH	You nick? Ooh-er ... what did you nick?
HAM	Nothing, cloth ears! The word is *unique* ... *(spells it out)* U N I Q U E.
JAPHETH	OK, Ham? Well, good old Dad! So you're unique.
NOAH	Not so much of the old! *(Clips JAPHETH round the ear)*
JAPHETH	God chose *you,* and you're unique.
NOAH	Yes, that's about it.
SHEM	But then I'm unique too – 'cos I'm taller than the rest of you.
HAM	And I'm unique 'cos I'm the eldest son.
JAPHETH	*(Not to be outdone)* And I'm unique because I'm ... *(Scratches his head wondering)*
SHEM AND HAM	You're unique because you're thick, cloth ears!
JAPHETH	But what about the animals? Are they unique? There's a pair of each, one male and one female.
NOAH	You've got it. Each animal is unique and each of their young is unique. Remember your two pet rabbits?

SHEM	Yes. Bred like rabbits; there are hundreds now ...
JAPHETH	And they are all different.
HAM	It's amazing! God must be very creative to make so much uniqueness ...
JAPHETH	Indeed! But what would you get if you crossed a sheep with a kangaroo?
SHEM AND HAM	*(Together)* A woolly jumper!
JAPHETH	And if you crossed a kangaroo with a zebra?
SHEM AND HAM	A stripey jumper!
JAPHETH	I'll try another. What would you get if you crossed an elephant with a mouse? *(Let the children answer and add other jokes)*
NOAH	And each one unique. And me? I'm the One and Only Captain Noah!

Story

You could use this story during **Exploring the Bible.** *This story emphasizes the Bible's message about Noah and why God chose him to begin the new age. It is an example of how the Bible story could be told. Remember that it is better to tell a story than read it.*

Who was Noah? Noah was an ordinary fellow. He had a wife, and three sons, Shem, Ham and Japheth. His sons had grown up and each had a wife of his own. Noah liked a drink, and sometimes he got carried away and had a pint too much. That's about all we know about Noah until one day when a great adventure began ...

To begin at the beginning: the world had started well. God made it. It was very good. The earth was beautiful with its many plants, animals and birds. There was such a variety of colours – all the colours of the rainbow. God had made man and woman and given them the job of caring for the earth and all its plants and creatures. But things began to go wrong. The world became a mess. There was violence everywhere. You were not safe in your own bed at night! People were selfish and jealous of one another. They fought among themselves. One day people would become so violent that they would be overwhelmed by their own evil. It would be like a huge wave that sweeps in across the sea shore and takes out into the ocean all the rubbish, leaving the beach clean again.

God was sad that people had become so selfish and were destroying the good earth. God decided that the earth and everyone on it must be destroyed, so that God could begin again. There would be a flood which would destroy the earth. It would be like turning over a spoilt page in a school exercise book and beginning on a fresh new page. But God so loved all that had been made that God could not destroy everything. Then God noticed Noah. Would Noah trust God? Could God work with Noah and begin again? God made a plan ...

God chose Noah. Noah seemed an honest and trustworthy person. God knew what Noah was like and God liked Noah. So God called Noah and asked him to build. Noah was to build an ark so that he, his wife and their three sons Shem, Ham and Japheth, their wives and a pair of each animal and bird would be kept safe when the flood of destruction came. After the flood Noah could help to build a new earth.

So it was that Noah, who was just like you and me, became the One and Only Captain Noah.

Songs

Theme Song: **The Rainbow Song** (see page 70)

'Who built the ark?' *Someone's Singing Lord No. 44*

'O the Lord looked down' *Alleluya! No. 72*

'Rise and shine' *Alleluya! No. 74* (Black)

Games

The theme of **Noah** emphasizes God's choice of Noah and Noah's trust in God. Choose games that reflect these concepts of choice, trust and following a leader.

For example:

> *Simon Says*
> *A blindfold game*
> *A trust game*

Creative Resources

Portraits

You will need:

- card in the shape of a face,
- felt tip pens,
- Copydex glue
- oddments of wool.

Ask a local portrait photographer if you could have the central pieces of card thrown away when photograph mounts are made. These make ideal sizes of card for self portraits. Strands of wool the appropriate colour can be added with Copydex to make hair.

Hand Puppets

You will need:

- wallpaper paste,
- newspaper,
- card (or the inside of a toilet roll),
- material oddments.

Make the heads of papier mâché and the bodies from fabric.

Cut the card 10 cms x 5cms. Roll it round your finger and glue to make a tube. Build papier mâché round this base for a head. Use screwed up dry paper and attach with strips of pasted paper to form the nose, ears, eye brows and other features. Leave to dry, then paint. Hair can be added by sticking wool on with glue. See the section **Craft Workshop** on page 67 for further details of how to make papier mâché.

Cut out two body shaped pieces of fabric. Decorate with other pieces of fabric and attach to the head.

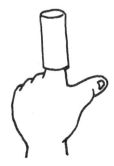 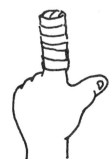 

Toilet Roll Puppet

Stuff a cardboard tube with paper. Add a face and make arms from curled paper – cut the ends to make fingers. Make beard, hair etc from scraps of wool, then dress the puppet, securing the head-dress with an elastic band.

Tape a stick to the inside back of the puppet. Hold the puppet behind a stage or table to make it perform.

Animal Puppets

These puppets are made from old socks. Add features made from buttons, sequins etc. Use copydex to attach scraps of fabric, felt and wool.

Practise using your hand to give the animal different expressions.

Models of Noah and family

You will need:

- newspaper,
- wallpaper paste,
- round balloons,
- dressmakers' dummies,
- old clothes.

Make heads from papier mâché and place on the neck of the dummy. Dressmakers' dummies can usually be borrowed from members of the congregation (or a friendly shop). Clothes, or borrowed lengths of dress fabric can be used to pin round the body.

Papier mâché heads are easy to make using the following tips:

Use a firm, round balloon. Put the balloon neck in a jam-jar and secure it. Grease the balloon with vaseline (Fig. 1). Cover in strips of paper soaked in paste (Fig. 2). Use a layer of white newsprint followed by a layer of coloured. (The *Financial Times* is pink).

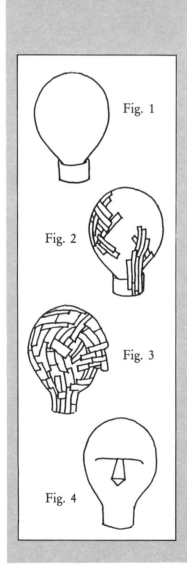

Fig. 1

Fig. 2

Fig. 3

Fig. 4

This results in even layers – you will need to put on about 5-7 (Fig. 3).

Allow to dry slowly. Burst the balloon and cut round the neck carefully so that it fits the neck of the dummy (Fig. 4). Secure the head and paint on the face.

Dress the character as suggested.

Body puppets

The more adventurous may like to try making their own bodies for the models!

For this you will need a sheet of corrugated cardboard twice the width and length of your own body. Fold it in two and cut a small hole in the fold, through which you can insert the papier mâché head (Fig. 5)

For each arm use a tube of card. Cut a V shape to create the elbow, bend and sellotape into position (Fig. 6). Cut out hands from the cardboard, push into the tube and glue into place.

Attach the arms to the body with strips of papier mâché. Stick the sides of the body together, using either sellotape or more strips of papier mâché (Fig. 7).

To make a base which will enable the figure to stand up you will need a large square cardboard box, such as those available from a supermarket. Cut down the middle of two opposite sides of the box, and cut a triangle out of the bottom (Fig. 8).

Overlap the cut sides and secure with a split pin. Make a slit in the other two sides of the box (Fig. 9).

Finally slot in your model body, and dress the figure.

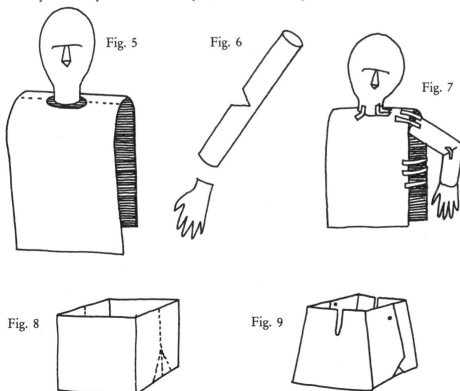

Fig. 5   Fig. 6   Fig. 7

Fig. 8   Fig. 9

GENESIS 6.14-22; 7.16

LEADER'S PREPARATION
Understanding the Bible

Before God destroyed the earth, Noah had been chosen to be the person through whom God's work of salvation would be resumed. Noah was called to build an ark without knowing why. He obediently began to build a ship of gigantic proportions in the middle of dry land, miles from the sea! Noah, his family and the animals assembled and God closed the door. The ark is the symbol of God's care as the earth returns to the chaos before creation. The emphasis in the passage is not on destruction but on the gracious provision of God.

Background material

The ark is a biblical symbol of a 'safe haven', a place of protection. Through the ark, God saves Noah and his family from the flood. Later the ark became the symbol of the Early Church. The ark set Christians apart from the power of the sinful world. It was a sanctuary from sin. Today the symbol of the ark is used as the logo of the World Council of Churches, though its meaning has changed. Now the emphasis is on the journey, as Christians of various denominations share the adventure of the Christian pilgrimage together.

Life is a challenging experience. There are times when we each feel the particular need for a 'safe haven' or a 'bolt hole', a place where we know we will be safe. This may be from physical danger – for example, seeking refuge in a dry community hall from a flooded home. It may be escape from emotional or social pressures, seeking a quiet place, or a person who will provide an opportunity to sort out the problem. We may seek safety from a welter of new knowledge or ideas, needing time to consider them before making a response.

Children and adolescents need a safe haven. They need to understand and reflect on their experiences in order to make sense of life. Children do this by creating dens; adolescents place a 'No Entry' sign on their bedroom doors. Dens are a type of sanctuary.

Image: The Ark

Objectives

☐ To introduce the children to the ark in the flood story.

☐ To help children see the ark as a safe place provided by God.

☐ To explore with children their need for a 'safe place'.

☐ To help children understand that God cares about their safety.

TEACHING MATERIAL

Rainbow Time 1

Sing the theme song on page 70, and others (see today's **Resources**). Introduce the image to the whole group in one of the following ways:

● The play (see page today's **Resources**).

● Dens – give several groups of children corrugated cardboard, pieces of wood, sheets of polythene, old sheets and blankets. Ask them to make a safe place (den) in which to live; let them comment on each other's efforts.

● Slides – show alternating slides of human disasters and places of safety (homes and families).

Group Activities 5-7 year olds

Sharing

Show pictures of children in safe places – for example: in bed, in the arms of a parent, in the child's tree house or den. Discuss with the children:

● the different places where they feel safe,

● what makes a place safe,

● the need for a safe place,

● the times when we need a safe place.

Exploring the Bible Genesis 6.14-22; 7.16

Tell the story of the building of the ark, how the animals were assembled in it and how God closed the ark door. Use the suggestions in today's **Resources** or the points below. You could tell the story with a refrain spoken by the children – for example: *Noah built the ark!*

- God asked Noah to build an ark miles from the sea,
- the neighbours made fun of Noah,
- Noah trusted in God,
- the ark provided a safe place for Noah's family and the animals,
- the ark had three decks, a roof and door,
- the ark was covered with tar inside and out,
- Noah collected the animals together,
- God closed the door.

Talking

Think about how Noah's ark was like a den. God was concerned to keep Noah and his family safe. God cares for us.

Creating

Choose one or more of the following options:

- ask the children to write about the places where they feel safe,
- make a collage or draw a picture of a den – it could include the special people allowed in,
- make a model of the ark using an empty shoe box (see today's **Creative Resources**),
- construct a large ark (with other groups), each group doing a deck (see today's **Creative Resources**),
- make animal faces or masks for the ark (see today's **Creative Resources**).

Group Activities 8-12 year olds

Sharing

Show pictures of dens, churches and the symbol of the World Council of Churches. Remind children that some people call the main part of their church building the nave (Latin 'navis' a ship).
Talk about:

- the ark as a symbol of the church,
- people using churches for protection or sanctuary from enemies,
- how we all need sanctuary,
- how dens provide sanctuary.

Exploring the Bible

Use the biblical material for the 5-7 year olds, adding the following:

- the ark as a symbol of God's care,
- the chaos which we create in the world,
- those animals and people shut outside the ark,
- how the emphasis is not on destruction but God's provision,
- how God provides for our needs.

Talking

Think about how a den is like the ark and the church. Explore why the ark was needed. Think about ways in which the children need protecting.

Creating

Choose one or more of the following options:

- make a den using cardboard boxes and polythene sheets,
- draw or write about the reasons for having a den,
- start or continue with the figures of Noah (see Monday's **Creative Resources**),
- construct an ark (see today's **Creative Resources**)
- make a model ark and some animals (see today's **Creative Resources**)

Rainbow Time 2

Use this time together to share what each group has made and discovered.

RESOURCES

These useful resources will help you in your planning. Select those which are most helpful in your particular situation.

Play

This play can be used in **Rainbow Time 1** to introduce your theme:

Hark? No, an Ark!

Characters: NOAH
NOAH'S WIFE
SHEM, HAM and JAPHETH
Various neighbours

An open space. Noah is looking up at the sky. He is joined by his wife.

WIFE	What a lovely day! Not a cloud in the sky ...
NOAH	Yes, I think it will be a busy day.
WIFE	Hmmmm ... there's the sheep to dip before shearing, the animals to feed, the dog to take for a walk ...
NOAH	Noooooh – I don't mean that kind of work!
WIFE	Well – what else?
NOAH	Promise you won't laugh and I'll tell you.
WIFE	Getting you up and working is a laugh itself! No, I won't laugh.
NOAH	Well, I'm going to build a boat ...
WIFE	*(Roars with laughter)* A boat for your bath? Haven't you got enough boats already?
NOAH	No. A big one – for all of us. Those three sons of ours – and a few animals ...
WIFE	You're joking of course!
NOAH	Oh, no I'm not! *(He holds up a card with these words and encourages the boys to join him)*
WIFE	Oh, yes you are! *(She holds up a card with her words and gets the girls to join in)*
	Each waves their arms to encourage their respective children to join in. It is repeated several times.
NOAH	*(To the girls)* Whose side are you on? That's quite enough! I'm building a boat. A large boat. An ark.
WIFE	'Hark', did you say?

NOAH	No – cloth ears! An *ark.*
WIFE	You've got your eyes shut! Haven't you noticed? There's no water here to sail a boat.
NOAH	I have to do it ...

Their three sons join Noah and his wife.

SHEM	What's to do, Dad?
NOAH	We're building a boat.
HAM	*A boat?*
NOAH	Yup – a boat.
JAPHETH	But there's no water! It's seven days walk north before you reach any ... *(He starts pacing it out)*
HAM	And a good fourteen days walk south. *(He too paces it out. They fall over one another being unable to decide north from south)*
SHEM	And west – well, maybe a walk of four days.
JAPHETH	And if you went east you'd just go on and on and on ... Anyway, what's this boat for? Is it a house-boat? A house-boat with a view of the desert?!

The neighbours join them.

NEIGHBOUR 1	What's all the noise about?
SHEM	Our Dad's building a boat.
NEIGHBOUR 1	Ha ha! You *are* joking of course?
SHEM	Oh, no he's not! *(Waves the children to join in again)*
Wife	Oh, yes he is! *(Waves the children to join in. Repeat several times.)*
NOAH	Shush, shush, shush!! Don't start *that* again!
NEIGHBOUR 1	You're mad! Where's the water? *(He looks up and down. Races around then finally says to the children)*
NEIGHBOUR 1	Have you seen any water?
NEIGHBOUR 2	Where has this mad idea come from?
NOAH	God told me there is to be a flood.
NEIGHBOUR 1	God! You mean your voices again. Look at the sky – there's been no rain for weeks!
NOAH	Well, I'm building. Will you help me?
NEIGHBOURS	*(Slinking away)* You must be joking! *(They go off signalling to the children that Noah is mad)*
NOAH	And what about you? You're my sons. Will you help?
SHEM	I suppose it will make a change.

HAM	It's not every one who gets the chance to build a boat round here!
JAPHETH	(Excitedly) Or live in a house boat ...
ALL THREE	*In the desert!*
NOAH	To work. We need trees to saw ...
HAM	I *saw* a tree. Was it yesterday?
	They all groan and get to work.
NOAH	We need gopher wood.
SHEM	*(To Ham)* Come on – go-for-wood, Dad said.
JAPHETH	But there isn't any wood.
NOAH	Cloth ears! The name of the wood is gopher. There's oak, or cedar, or olive wood – but we need gopher. It's good, strong wood and that's what God needs for this ark. So get a move on!

Story

You could use this story during **Exploring the Bible.** *This part of the story tells of God's command to build an ark. It demonstrates how God cares for us and provides a safe place for us. It is an example of how the Bible story could be told. Remember that it is better to tell a story than to read it.*

Noah seemed a good sort - a trusting sort of fellow in God's eyes. The world had been spoilt by people's selfishness. God wanted to destroy the world and begin again. But God could not bear to destroy the beautiful earth. God loved creation. Then God saw Noah. God decided to save Noah and through him and his family, to make a new beginning.

A place was needed where Noah and his family could be safe. A pair of each sort of animal and bird would also be needed for the fresh start. God had a plan. A safe place could be built - an ark - and Noah would be the builder! The ark would need to be large enough to house comfortably all the creatures and save them from the flood of destruction overcoming the world.

Noah began to build. It was like a floating house -boat, but miles from the sea. No wonder the neighbours laughed! Noah persisted - he trusted God. There were to be three decks and a door in the side, God had said. It was to be made from good timber and, as if that was not enough, it was to be coated inside and out with tar to make it waterproof. It was a huge undertaking, but eventually it was finished. There was still no sign of water, not the tiniest raindrop.

Noah realised that the animal crew would need food. He had to find enough food of the right sort for each animal - after all, he didn't want them getting hungry and eating one another! Then he had to round up the animals and birds - no easy task! They didn't see the point. Where was the rain? Noah trusted still and thanked God that they would have a safe place whenever the flood began. When all the animals were safely in the ark, Noah gathered together his family. There was still no sign of rain. Noah began to feel rather silly. Had he imagined that God had spoken to him? Had he imagined the instructions to build the ark? Then he heard a bang. It was the door. God had closed it. It was tightly shut. A moment later everyone heard the rain begin ...

Songs

Theme Song: **The Rainbow Song** (see page 70)

'He's got the whole world in his hands' *Come and Praise No. 20*

'Who built the ark?' *Someone's singing Lord No. 44*

'I watch the sunrise' *Alleluya! No. 15*

'Put your hand in the hand' *Alleluya! No. 50*

Games

The theme of the ark emphasizes the idea of God's provision of sanctuary. Choose games that reflect this concept. For example:

Sardines; A child ('it') is sent to hide while the remaining players close their eyes. On a given signal they begin to search for 'it', joining 'it' in hiding. Gradually all the children are huddled together like sardines, safe in sanctuary.

Creative Resources

Collage of the ark

You will need:

- end rolls of newsprint (or old white sheets),
- powder paint (red, yellow, blue and brown),
- wide brushes or sponges.

Decide the size of the finished ark according to the space available or the number of children working on the project. Create decks, port holes and stalls for the animals – don't forget the door! Position the self-portraits you made on Monday as faces looking out of the port-holes. Later you could add animals in proportion to the ark. (Instructions for making large model animals appear in the **Craft Workshop** section on page 67.) Paint with wide brushes, or use sponges to obtain a stippled effect. Hang on a wall.

Alternatively, draw a bold, simple outline of the ark using the enlarged template overleaf. Fill in the outlines by sticking on screwed up tissue paper.

If you feel really adventurous, try creating a three-dimensional ark using large cardboard boxes from the local supermarket!

Template for Ark Collage

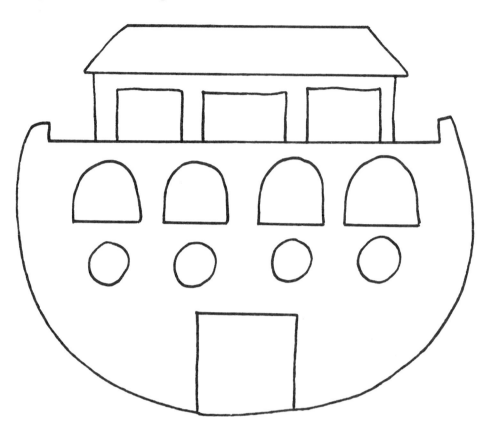

Animal faces

You will need:

- card plates,
- newspaper,
- wallpaper paste,
- powder paint,
- thin elastic.

Use the card plates as a base and build up with strips of papier mâché. Features can be added using balls or strips of dry paper held in position with sticky paper. Slide or dip strips of paper in paste. Dry faces gradually, for example in an airing cupboard. When dry, faces can be painted with powder paint and varnished. Attach the elastic on each side of the face and across the back of the mask so that it can be worn.

Model ark and animals

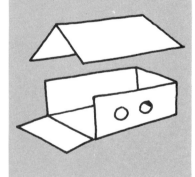

You will need:

- an empty shoe box,
- a piece of card twice the width of the box (for the roof),
- scissors, glue, paint, pencils.

Cut the two short ends of the shoe box to form gang-planks (see diagram). Fold the piece of card to make a roof – grass or straw could be stuck to this – then paint your ark. Instructions for making model animals appear under **Craft Workshop** on page 67.

GENESIS 7.11-24

LEADER'S PREPARATION
Understanding the Bible

The writer tells us of the heavens opening and the rain beginning. The word 'flood' is also used in the creation story where it is translated as 'the firmament above'. The ancient peoples believed that there was a huge dome over the earth which held back the waters of a heavenly ocean. During the flood this firmament was released and waters deluged down upon the earth. The boundaries of the oceans on the earth's surface were also 'freed' so there was a return to the chaos before creation. It was terrifying. The natural orders fixed by God's word were no more. There was no separation between heaven and earth, the waters above and those below.

It is important to note the nature of God as revealed through the writer's story. God's power and freedom allow the world to be engulfed by chaos, drowning human sin. Judgment is there but God ensures creation's salvation by providing for the preservation of Noah and his family as representatives of humanity.

With children, the emphasis should not be on the destruction of the bad, but on the way God speaks to Noah, and enables him to respond to this call, so that God's intention for creation can be fulfilled.

Background material

Water is fundamental to our existence. In the womb we are surrounded and protected by water. Our bodies are 90% water. Clean, safe drinking water is a basic human need. Until a drought, or a burst water main, we may be unaware of our dependence on this everyday commodity.

Water is used as a powerful symbol in religion, but it is ambiguous. It is a symbol of life but also of death. The Jewish idea of heaven found in the vision of John in *Revelation* says 'and the sea vanished', *(Revelation 21.1 GNB)*. The Jews of the biblical period were land dwellers and for them the sea represented fear and tempest. It must be remembered that for much of their history they had no coast line. Water was used by the Jews for ritual purification, a practice which was taken up by the early church in the rite of baptism. Christians 'wash away' their old life in the waters of baptism and are raised up to a new life. *1 Peter 3.20* likens baptism to the flood experience.

Children use water everyday. They are aware that water cleanses and that it gives life. Using this daily experience, parallels can be drawn with the flood story.

Image: Water

Objectives

☐ To tell the story of the flood water.

☐ To explore water in everyday life.

☐ To help children understand the use of water as a symbol.

☐ To understand water as both life giving and life destroying.

TEACHING MATERIAL

Rainbow Time 1

Display the rainbow symbol of the holiday club.
Sing the theme song (page 70) and other songs (see today's **Resources**).
Introduce the image for today to the whole group in one of the following ways:

● The play (see today's **Resources**).

● Set up several 'experiments' to explore the use of water. Ask the children what is likely to happen in each of these cases:

  – Take two vases and fill one with water. Put a flower in each.

  – Take two bowls of identical size and put a cupful of dried peas or beans in each. Pour three cups of water into one of the bowls.

  – Put some dried milk powder into two cups. Give them to two children, but only allow one child to add water!

● Listen to a piece of music about water – for example: 'La Mer' by Debussy or 'The Fish' from *Carnival of the Animals* by Saint-Saens. Ask the children how they felt when listening

Group Activities 5-7 year olds

Sharing

Collect pictures of water being used in the home and the community. For example: advertisements for toothpaste, washing-machines, baths, showers and swimming pools. Talk about the pictures. Discuss:

● water used for cleaning bodies and clothes,
● water for drinking,
● water for cooking vegetables,
● water for leisure; swimming, skating, boating, waterskiing.

Exploring the Bible Genesis 7.11-24

Tell the story of the flood waters rising. Use the suggestions in today's **Resources** or the points below. You could tell the story with a refrain spoken by the children – for example: *The waters rose...*

- God shut the door and it started to rain,
- the flood began submerging houses,
- finally, even the tree-tops disappeared,
- the ark began to float,
- Noah, his family and the animals were safe inside the ark,
- after forty days and nights the rain stopped,
- outside the ark everything was fresh and new.

Talking

Talk about positive experiences such as a rain storm that cleans the pavements, or how after a hot day or exercise we are refreshed by a cool bath.

Creating

Choose one or more of the following options:

- draw a picture of your favourite belongings and circle the three you would take if there was a flood,
- make a zig zag book of drawings showing how water is used,
- imagine being in a flood; act out your feelings as you watch the waters rise, wait for rescue, and are taken to safety,
- use reference books to discover where rain comes from. Make a chart to illustrate the rain cycle,
- run a sheet of paper under water and paint a picture on it.

Group Activities 8-12 year olds

Sharing

Collect pictures of water used for washing: for example advertisements for washing powder, washing machines, car washes, baths and showers. Include a picture of a *font* or *baptistry*. Talk about how:

- water is used for washing,
- water is used for cleaning and making new,
- water is a symbol of new life,
- baptism is a symbol of washing away the old life and giving new life.

Exploring the Bible

Use the biblical material for the 5-7 year olds adding the following:

- God's sadness over sin,
- God's desire to recreate the world,
- the flood destroys,
- the flood brings new life.

Talking

Talk about how the flood cleansed the earth. Discuss other flood stories (see today's **Resources**).

Creating

Choose one of the following options:

- make a booklet to show how water is important to us,
- create a poster to advertise safety in water,
- do some experiments to discover how much water different materials absorb – for example: a piece of cotton material, sponge, plastic, wood, foil. Record your results on a bar graph,

- imagine you are in the ark and write a poem about your feelings as the flood waters rise,
- write a collection of flood stories – include one that you have made up (see today's **Resources**).

Rainbow Time 2

Use this time together to share what each group has made and discovered.

RESOURCES

These useful resources will help you in your planning. Select those which are most helpful in your particular situation.

Play

This play can be used in **Rainbow Time 1** to introduce your theme:

Water, Water, Everywhere

Characters:	Noah
	Mrs Noah
	Shem, Ham and Japheth, their sons
	Three Wives

Inside the Ark.

NOAH	Listen! It's raining. Thank goodness I built the ark.
SHEM	*You* built the ark? What about me? I helped – and I have the blisters to prove it!
HAM	And me! I helped – look at the cuts on my hands.
JAPHETH	Hey! Don't forget all the tar I painted on the hull. I still smell of it – pooh!
MRS NOAH	When is this rain going to stop, Noah? I want to hang the washing out. All your smelly socks are washed and I need to get them dry.
NOAH	When is the rain going to stop? Well, it certainly won't stop today ...
MRS NOAH	Well, Mr Weatherman, will it be fine tomorrow?
NOAH	No, it will rain tomorrow – and the next day and the next.
MRS NOAH	What is going on outside? Can I go out?
NOAH	Certainly – but don't forget to take your snorkel! Don't you remember about the flood?
SHEM	Flood ... flood? Oh, the *flood!* Yes, that's why we built the ark isn't it?
HAM	I remember.
JAPHETH	Flood did you say? What flood? I want to go out and play football!
SHEM	Nincompoop! Surely you remember the flood. God told Dad to build the ark to protect us and keep us safe. If you want to play football, you'll have to swim for the ball.
JAPHETH	Swim? You know I can't swim. I get seasick in the bath. Anyway, I don't believe you about a flood.
HAM	Go and look out of the porthole then, Japheth. You'll see!

JAPHETH goes off, then comes rushing back.

JAPHETH	Help! Ham's right, there is a flood. What are we going to do?
NOAH	Nothing. We are going to do absolutely nothing.
JAPHETH	But what about our home? The waters are still rising – they'll cover the house!
NOAH	It doesn't matter. The ark is our home now. There's plenty of food for everyone and plenty of work to be done.
SHEM	More work? Huh! I thought we'd finished with that once the ark was built.
NOAH	The animals must be mucked out and fed. Do you remember all the food we stowed on the ark? You asked why there was so much – well, now you know. There's three decks so there's plenty of room for everyone.
	The wives come rushing in.
WIFE 1	Noah! You didn't tell us that there were mice on this trip!
NOAH	Oh, yes – there's a pair of each animal.
WIFE 2	That will be cosy. One of each?
NOAH	Yes. That's the point.
WIFE 3	But they'll ... they'll **multiply**.
NOAH	Only if they know their two times table!
WIVES	Perhaps we'll give the trip a miss.
NOAH	You're here now, and so are the mice. Make the most of it! Perhaps you'll get to like them.
JAPHETH	Listen – the rain is getting heavier.
SHEM	The flood waters have reached the tops of the trees. Soon they'll be covered and disappear.
JAPHETH	*(Starts chanting)* Rain, rain, go away; come again another day.
	He encourages the children to join in.
JAPHETH	Why can't it stop? Why do we need all this rain?
NOAH	We need rain to drink and to wash with.
SHEM	*(Interrupts)* I can easily do without a wash.
WIFE 1	You don't mind ...
WIFE 2	But we do!
WIFE 3	Without a bath you'll smell worse than the skunk!
NOAH	Your mother needs water to wash your socks. We need water to grow plants or you will starve.
JAPHETH	OK, Dad – we need water! But why so much?
NOAH	It will make everything clean again. You've seen all the evil and violence on the earth. Well, the evil will be submerged by the waters. They will drown all that is evil and bad. We will be able to make a new start.
JAPHETH	A fresh start. Hmm, that sounds good. The earth will be clean and new.

SHEM	Did you feel anything then?
JAPHETH	It felt as if the ark was moving!
SHEM	Yes – there's nothing except water beneath us! We're afloat!
NOAH	Well, from now on I must be Captain Noah and you must be my crew. So get to work. *(Indicating the children)* And you!
WIVES	It's water, water everywhere.
HAM	Listen to the rain – it's pouring down ...
JAPHETH	I think I'm going to be sea sick!

He rushes off.

Story

You could use this part of the story during **Exploring the Bible.** *It tells of the flood which destroys the world yet brings Noah to safety to begin a new age. It is an example of how the Bible story could be told. Remember that it is better to tell a story than to read it.*

Noah was inside the ark with his wife, his sons Shem, Japheth and Ham and their wives. Also in the ark was a pair of every bird and animal – from the desert gerbil to the roaring lion. A place was found for everyone and they all settled down to rest. The ark shook as the door closed. God had shut and fixed it tightly.

Gradually, the sky darkened. Everyone became rather quiet. Some of the passengers were a little bit frightened! Noah knew that whatever happened God had provided for them all. Then the rain began ...

The downpour increased until it sounded as if the heavens had opened over their heads and were pouring down on them! Soon the earth was covered as rivers burst their banks and rose to join one another. As the flood rose, houses and villages disappeared. Finally, even the treetops could be seen no more. The hills were flattened beneath an ocean of water. Suddenly the ark started to roll. There was silence within. The ark was moving and they were afloat. Everyone knew what this meant – there was nothing but water beneath them!

Outside the ark was darkness – no sound but the water lapping against the side of the ark and the rain pouring down. Noah and his family were glad that God had provided for them. The tar, which had been so difficult to put on the boards, now kept the ark waterproof so that it was warm and dry inside.

It rained and it rained, for so long that the family and the animals almost stopped noticing it. Life took on a pattern. There was not much space for so many, but there was enough to eat and a warm place to sleep. Then, after about forty days, there was a shout. 'Listen everybody!' the voice echoed through the ark. Nothing. Silence. It had stopped raining!

Noah knew that he must wait for God's instructions. Outside the ark everything was fresh and new. Noah knew that the evil had been destroyed and that God had made a new beginning. He had been given a second chance. Everything was clean and pure – exactly like the world had been at the beginning.

Songs

Theme Song: **The Rainbow Song** (see page 70)

'Water of Life' *Come and Praise No. 2*

'You can't stop rain' *Come and Praise 2 No. 102*

'It's the springs' *Come and Praise 2 No. 82*

'O Lord, all the world belongs to you' *Come and Praise BBC No. 39*

'Let the Water flow' *The Oxford Assembly Book page 54*

Poem

'The history of the flood' *The Oxford Assembly Book page 128*

Games

The theme of water emphasizes its significance. Choose games that reflect this theme – for example:

Islands: The islands are made from large double sheets of newspaper placed on the floor. The floor is the sea. The children move around in the sea while music is played, but when it stops, sanctuary must be found from the flood waters on the islands. Gradually, the islands are made smaller and the children have to stand closer and closer together to be saved. Children who fall into the sea are out of the game.

Flood Stories

Examples of some of the stories from other cultures:

A North American Indian Story

Some Native Americans believe in a god called Bochica who gave them their laws. These laws were gradually disobeyed and ignored. Another god flooded the country until Bochica appeared as a rainbow and sent the rays of the sun to dry up the water and make an outlet to carry away the flood to the sea. Later, he divided the world into four parts and gave responsibility to each of four chiefs, who from that time saw that the laws were obeyed.

A Rainbow Story from India

The rainbow is the war bow of Indra, the warrior-king of the heavens, god of war and storms. His weapons are the thunderbolt and lightning, and the rainbow is his bow of war, which he laid aside after defeating the demons in a contest.

A Greek Legend

The goddess of the rainbow is Iris. She is the swift, bright messenger of the gods, who links the heavens with the earth.

More stories can be found in:
Gods and Men – Myths and Legends from the World's Religions by John Bailey
(*Myths and Legends series*, Oxford University Press)

Creative resources

Water experiment

You will need:
- a measuring jug,
- water,
- several different types of material.

Pour water gently from a measuring jug onto the different sorts of material. Stop when it appears that the material will not absorb any more water. Remember to note the level in the jug before you start and again when you finish. Record your results on a bar chart.

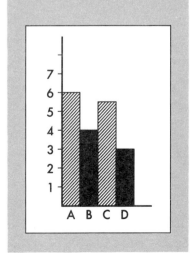

GENESIS 8. 1-5, 8-12

LEADER'S PREPARATION
Understanding the Bible

The ark containing Noah, his family and the animals came to rest on a mountain top. The writer uses a pun on the name *Noah* since the word for 'rest' – *nuach* – derives from the same root word as the name *Noah*. The rain ceased, God's wind blew and the flood began to subside. After the chaos of destruction God gave the earth peace. Noah sent out a dove to discover how far the water still extended. Finding no resting place, she returned. A week later Noah sent her out again. This time she returned carrying an olive twig in her beak. Tree-tops had begun to appear above the receding water! The dove was sent a third time; this time she did not return. At last she had found a place to nest.

It is God who tells Noah to leave the ark, not Noah's decision. Noah is the representative of the old order that is submerged beneath the flood-waters with all that violated God's creation. He is also the beginning of the *new* creation. The emphasis throughout is on the graciousness of God, who, having freed the earth from chaos now begins the new order ...

Background material

Both the dove and olive branch are symbols of peace – birds are also Christian symbols of renewal. They occur in the story as the flood ends and new life begins. The new life after the flood is to be a life lived at peace with God and in harmony with all creation. In everyday speech we talk about bringing peace into a situation by offering an offended friend 'an olive branch'. We are reminded that offering an olive branch is not an easy option, rather it costs effort, time, and thought. Jesus taught 'Happy are those who work for peace' *(Matthew 5.9 GNB)*

Often we are overwhelmed by our own sin. Sin is like a flood. In our acts of worship we confess before God. We acknowledge that we fail to care for others, we actively wrong them and thus sin against God who is present in our neighbour. The confession is followed by an assurance of God's forgiveness allowing us to make a new beginning. In many churches the confession and absolution are followed by the 'peace', symbolised by the friendly greeting of each other. Peace is God's gift to us.

Children know when things are not right in their relationships. They know their need of forgiveness and peace. Children need to be assured that they can make a new beginning.

Image: The Dove

Objectives

☐ To relate the story of the dove in the Noah story.

☐ To introduce the idea of the dove as a symbol.

☐ To see how the dove is used as a symbol of peace.

☐ To help children explore their need for peace and the ways they receive it.

TEACHING MATERIAL

Rainbow Time 1

Display the rainbow symbol. Sing the theme song, (see page 70) and others, including some from previous sessions. Introduce the image to the whole group in one of the following ways:

● the play (see today's **Resources**),

● slides or video of birds in flight,

● short talk by a bird watcher to include showing their binoculars, note-pad, sketch books etc.,

● information about the junior branch of the Royal Society for the Protection of Birds.

Group Activities 5-7 year olds

Sharing

Show a picture of children fighting. Talk about the occasions when participants have been involved in a fight, then discuss:

● fights over a toy or game,

● bullying,

● why people fight and how peace can be restored,

● difficulty of reconciliation.

Exploring the Bible Genesis 8.1-5, 8-12

Continue the story from yesterday. Use the suggestions in today's **Resources** or the points below. You could tell the story with a refrain spoken by the children – for example: *The earth was at peace.*

- the ark stopped drifting,
- the storm was over, peace returned,
- Noah sent out a dove – she returned exhausted,
- a week later the dove was sent out again,
- she returned carrying an olive branch,
- a week later the dove was sent a third time,
- this time she did not return,
- the earth was at peace after the flood.

Talking

Think of reasons for the association of the dove with peace. Help the children to remember times when they have a row with a friend and how peace was restored.

Creating

Choose one or more of the following options:

- make a bird mobile (see today's **Creative Resources**),
- draw a picture of a dove. Make it three-dimensional by cutting out paper in petal shapes and sticking them on in rows to create feathers and wings,

- find and mount magazine pictures to show ways in which people harm one another. Create a second sheet which shows people working peacefully together,
- make a booklet titled *Peace is ...*. This could show, for example, children sharing a favourite toy,
- paint a picture of the dove returning with the olive branch.

Group Activities 8-12 year olds

Sharing

Show a picture of a dove with an olive branch – for example: the symbol of Christian CND, or the picture in this book. Talk about why the dove is used. Discuss:

- the dove and the olive branch as symbols of peace,
- the role played by the United Nations in resolving disputes.

Exploring the Bible

Use the biblical material for 5-7 year olds adding the following:

- the waters receded,
- the tree tops were revealed,
- the dove found a resting place.

Talking

Talk about the dove and the olive branch as symbols of peace. Think about the occasions when we 'fall out' with our friends and how peace can be restored.

Creating

Choose one or more of the following options:

- make some bird mobiles or kites to suspend in a display (see today's **Creative Resources**),
- design a poster for the Royal Society for the Protection of Birds, to recruit new members,
- imagine you are a bird and describe your life,
- think of situations of conflict among your family and friends, and act them out in groups. Get those watching to suggest ways in which peace could be brought about,
- cut out newspaper headlines to show war makers and peace makers.

Rainbow Time 2

Use this time together to share what each group has made and discovered.

RESOURCES

These useful resources will help you in your planning. Select those which are most helpful in your particular situation.

Play

This play can be used in **Rainbow Time 1** to introduce your theme.

Bird of Peace?

Characters:	Noah
	Mrs Noah
	Shem, Ham and Japheth – their sons

Inside the ark at daybreak. Mr and Mrs NOAH are wandering up and down. One by one they are joined by their yawning sons. A cockerel crows off-stage.

HAM	*(Rubbing his eyes)* Another day! Why does that pesky cockerel have to wake so early?
JAPHETH	Yes, he wakes me up as well. Once he starts, all the others get going ...
SHEM	It's the dawn chorus.
JAPHETH	More like the carnival of the animals!
HAM	What's he got to crow about, anyway? You can hardly tell it's another morning. There's nothing new, just the same routine day after day ...
JAPHETH	Mucking out, putting fresh straw around, feeding the animals, clearing space for the birds to test their wings. And the next day what happens?
SHEM AND HAM	Mucking out, putting fresh straw around, feeding the animals ...
NOAH	Okay, okay – I know. It's the same for all of us.
HAM	And the rain goes on and on and on ... When will it ever stop?
SHEM	The animals are getting fretful. If you don't do something soon, Dad, they'll begin to fight ...
HAM	*(Waving a card with the words written on so that he encourages the boys to join him)* Oh, yes they will!
JAPHETH	*(Waving a card to the girls)* Oh, no they won't!
NOAH	*(To the children)* Here – who asked you to join in?
HAM	I did! *(Waves card again)*
JAPHETH	I did! *(Waves card)*
	HAM and JAPHETH start hitting one another with the cards in a mock battle.

NOAH	Stop it, both of you! *(He blows a whistle and signals them to stand at either side of him)* If you don't pack it in I'll take your names. *(Noah licks a pencil and starts to write)*
JAPHETH	Don't be silly. You know us!
	SHEM comes up and attempts to add some sanity to the occasion.
SHEM	It's the birds that I feel sorry for. There's so little room for them to spread their wings.
HAM	The owl is never sure if it's day or night.
JAPHETH	He sounds like a regular twit. *(Imitates the owl's call)*
HAM	What's the name of the bird that coos?
JAPHETH	Cooo – eeee!
HAM	Silly! You know what I mean. That white bird.
SHEM	Oh, the dove?
HAM	Yes, the dove. Whenever there's a row, the dove seems to understand. She flutters down among the arguing animals and brings a sense of peace, so that they stop fighting.
SHEM	You've been in the ark too long! Your imagination's getting the better of you.
HAM	No, Shem, I really believe it. Her colour is a symbol of peace.
SHEM	The dove a symbol of peace? You should see her and her mate fighting with the other birds to claim their bit of roof-space!
HAM	Well, I think she's peaceful. Perhaps it's because she has white feathers. She's certainly not like those sparrows – always squabbling!
JAPHETH	Or that vain peacock who has no time for anyone else.
	They continue arguing between themselves about the different birds.
NOAH	Let's have a bit of peace from you lot.
MRS NOAH	Listen everyone! Has anyone noticed anything? While you have been arguing, it's stopped.
NOAH	What's stopped?
MRS NOAH	The rain, of course!
ALL	You're right – it's stopped!
	There are cheers all round. The three sons leap about in excitement.
NOAH	Let's send out the dove, our bird of peace to explore the peaceful new world ...
MRS NOAH	Yes, the dove is the best one to send.

Story

You could use this story during **Exploring the Bible** *to emphasize the dove as a symbol of peace. It is an example of how the Bible story could be told. Remember that it is better to tell a story than read it.*

The ark had stopped rolling. It seemed strange to be still at last after all the movement. Why had they stopped? Some of the animals thought they were stuck on the top of a mountain, and that was why the ark had come to rest. They had been squabbling among themselves because they were bored, but now they began to discuss what would happen next. Peace returned to the ark.

Outside the ark a new sound could be heard – it was like breathing. Was it God breathing, like the beginning of time when God breathed over the face of the waters? Was it a gentle breeze? Below was a new earth, cleansed of the violence and cruelty that had filled it.

The wind became stronger, the water level dropped and the sides of the ark began to steam as the timbers began to dry. All was peaceful inside and out.

Was it safe to venture out? How would anyone know if it was safe? Noah decided to investigate. He knew that sailors usually sent out a bird, since a bird could fly over the surface of the water. Noah was now a sailor – the One and Only Captain Noah – so he chose a dove and sent her off.

When the dove returned she was weak with exhaustion. She had found nowhere to rest above the surface of the water. Everyone would have to be patient and wait.

A week went by. The crew began to get restless again, so Noah sent the dove out a second time. All eyes were on her as she flew up and disappeared over the horizon. Hours went past. The animals got tired of waiting and dozed off. The fluttering of wings, and Noah's cry, woke everyone from sleep. The dove had returned – but this time it was different.

Quickly the news spread around the ark. The dove had brought back an olive leaf! Where had it come from? Peace had returned to the earth. The flood was getting lower, for trees had re-appeared ...

Another week passed, and the dove was sent out for a third time. Everyone waited, but by nightfall she had not returned. When day broke the next morning she had still not appeared. She was not coming back. She had found a new home.

A new life was beginning.

Songs

Theme Song: **The Rainbow Song** (see page 70)

'O Lord, all the world belongs to you' *Come and Praise No. 39*

'Peace, perfect peace' *Come and Praise No. 53*

'Let there be peace on earth' *Alleluya! No. 42*

'Make me a channel of thy peace' *Alleluya! No. 43*

'Peace is flowing like a river' *Alleluya! No. 48*

'If I had a hammer' *Someone's Singing, Lord No. 37*

Games

The theme of the dove emphasizes the idea of peace makers. One of the ways we show that we are at peace with others is by working together. Choose games that reflect this concept. Play, for example, some games where the children need to cooperate with one another:

- a three-legged race,
- a wheelbarrow race,
- blind-fold led through an obstacle course.

Creative resources

Bird mobile 1

You will need:

- thin card,
- pencil,
- scissors,
- tissue or crepe paper,
- a ruler,
- glue or staples,
- cotton thread.

Cut the shape of the bird's body from card (Fig. 1). Fold a sheet of paper into a concertina shape, make a vertical slit in the body and thread the folded paper through the cut. Fan the paper out to look like wings.

Cut strips of crepe or tissue paper for the tail, curling them around scissors or a ruler (Fig. 2). Stick or staple the tail into place (Fig. 3). Colour the mobile, and attach a piece of cotton thread to hang it up.

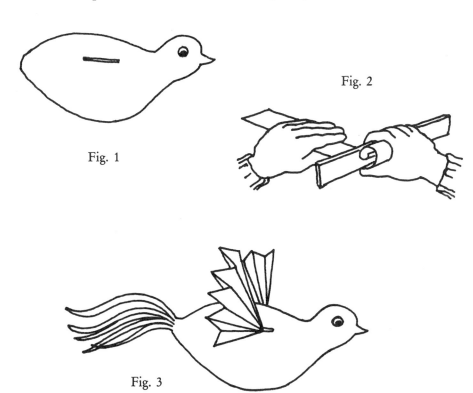

Fig. 2

Fig. 1

Fig. 3

Bird mobile 2

You will need:

- thin card or thick paper,
- pencil,
- scissors,
- staples or glue,
- a ruler,

Cut two strips of card 2cm wide; make one 15cm in length and the other 25cm. Place the short strip on top of the long one and cut one end into a point for the beak (Fig. 4).

Form the short strip into a loop to make the head and glue or staple. Form the longer strip into a body the same way (Fig. 5). Cut a small strip for the eye (Fig. 6).

Now cut strips of various lengths to make a tail (Fig. 7). Curl the tail-feathers as in Fig. 8, staple the tail to the body and attach cotton to hang the mobile up (Fig. 8).

Fig. 4

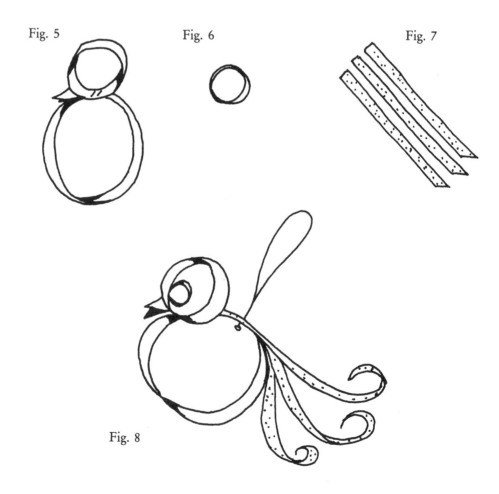

Fig. 5   Fig. 6   Fig. 7

Fig. 8

GENESIS 8.20-22; 9.8-17

LEADER'S PREPARATION
Understanding the Bible

The flood marked the end of one era and the beginning of a new one. God had wiped out sinful creation and saved a remnant to become a new creation. There was a need for a new agreement relating God and humanity; the Bible word is covenant. God promised henceforth to be faithful to humanity and never to destroy the earth again. The symbol of this new covenant was the rainbow.

There are many 'rainbow' stories in ancient cultures written to explain this natural phenomenon in the heavens. The Genesis story of the rainbow has a deeper meaning for it is a sign of the constancy and love of God. The Hebrew word for 'rainbow' means 'bow of war'; the writer is showing that God has laid aside the bow of war and will never again destroy the earth. The stability of nature is assured, reflecting the blessing and sustenance of God. Whatever humanity does, God is committed to creation.

While the earth remains, seed-time and harvest, cold and heat, summer and winter, day and night, shall not cease. *(Genesis 8.22)*

The rainbow is the sign of a covenant which God initiates, linking heaven and earth in God's saving and preserving grace.

Background Material

The Old Testament covenants between God and the Jews were based on the belief that God expected certain responses, such as obedience, honour and just dealings, from the people. In return God gave favour, protection and blessing.

In daily life we make *promises* to one another – for example, to trust a friend. If one of us fails to honour that promise, apologies are needed to prevent a breakdown in the relationship. Countries similarly make *treaties* which are to the mutual benefit of each side. These examples are all illustrations of the biblical word 'covenant'.

Children need to know that the promises we make to them will be kept; that their world is reliable and predictable. They need to be able to recognise around them the continual signs of God's presence and goodwill.

Image: The Rainbow

Objectives

- [ ] To tell the story of the rainbow in the flood story.

- [ ] To understand the rainbow as a symbol of God's promises.

- [ ] To develop a scientific and religious understanding of the rainbow.

- [ ] To explore the use of the rainbow in the flood story.

TEACHING MATERIAL

Rainbow Time 1

Today, do not display your rainbow symbol. Instead, have ready a strip of material in each colour of the rainbow to display during the introduction. Sing the theme song (page 70) and other songs (see today's **Resources**)
Introduce the image to the whole group in one of the following ways:

- the play (see today's **Resources**)

- recall the order of the seven colours of the rainbow. As each colour is mentioned, produce the strip of material in the appropriate colour. Display them together so that a rainbow is formed. Learn one of the rhymes which help you to remember the order of the colours – for example: 'Richard of York gave battle in vain' – red, orange, yellow, green, blue, indigo, violet.

- Hold a colour competition. Divide the children into groups and give each group pencil and paper. Ask them to list ten objects of each colour of the rainbow. Give them a time-limit – and don't worry if some groups don't finish.

Group Activities 5-7 year olds

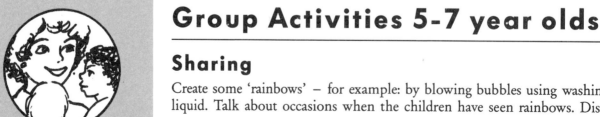

Sharing

Create some 'rainbows' – for example: by blowing bubbles using washing-up liquid. Talk about occasions when the children have seen rainbows. Discuss:

- the conditions necessary for rainbows,

- rain and sun,

- how the rainbow is like a 'bridge' from heaven to earth.

Exploring the Bible Genesis 8.20-22; 9.8-17

Tell the story of the new beginning with the rainbow as a reminder of God's promise. Use the suggestions in today's **Resources** or the points below. You could tell the story with a refrain spoken by the children – for example: *God keeps promises.*

- Noah gave thanks to God for his safety,

- everything was new and fresh,

- it was a new creation; a new beginning,

- God promised never to flood the earth again,

- the rainbow is a sign of God's promise.

Talking

Talk about the promises we make and the difficulty in keeping them. God *always* keeps promises.

Creating

Choose one or more of the following options:

- make a rainbow booklet with each page a different colour of the rainbow. Decorate the book with cut out pictures of objects of the appropriate colour,

- paint a large rainbow to hang in the church,

- weave a 'New Creation' (see today's **Creative Resources**),

- make some 'rainbow wristbands' (see today's **Creative Resources**),

- create some rainbows – for example: bubbles, oil on water.

Group Activities 8-12 year olds

Sharing

Experiment with light and a polished wine-glass to see how a rainbow is formed. Talk about other times when the group have seen rainbows. (Science books from the children's section of your local library will be helpful here.) Discuss:

- scientific explanations,

- refraction of light,

- why rainbows occur when there is sun and rain together.

Exploring the Bible

Use the biblical material for 5-7 year olds adding the following:

- the meaning of the word *rainbow* – 'God's bow of war',

- the promise of God is called a *covenant,*

- a covenant is an agreement between two partners,
- God makes the covenant; we break it when we sin,
- God remains faithful to the covenant,
- God keeps promises.

Talking

Look again at some of the stories written to explain the rainbow (see Wednesday's **Resources**). Discuss how these stories, and scientific explanations of the refraction of light, complement each other.

Creating

Choose one or more of the following options:

- use reference books to collect other stories written to explain the rainbow,
- discover how light is refracted to produce a rainbow, and make a chart of your findings,
- write a poem about the rainbow,
- make posters or banners to show the continued signs of God's promises – for example: the seasons. Include a rainbow in each,
- copy *Genesis 8.22* as a sentence from an illuminated manuscript.

Rainbow Time 2

Use this time together to share what each group has made and discovered.

RESOURCES

These useful resources will help you in your planning. Select those which are most helpful in your particular situation.

Play

This play can be used in **Rainbow Time 1** to introduce your theme.

The Rainbow of Promise

Characters: Noah (balding)
Mrs Noah (padded with cushions to look fat)
Ham, Shem, Japheth – their sons
Three wives

Noah and Mrs Noah are strolling along arm in arm.

NOAH   We've been together now for ... how long is it?

MRS NOAH   More years than I care to remember!

NOAH   And it doesn't seem a day too long.

MRS NOAH   Yes, I can even remember when you had hair!

NOAH   And I can remember when you were slim! Remember the promises we made to each other? To stay in the same place and have a quiet life? Now look where it's got us!

MRS NOAH   You're a land-lubber turned sailor.

NOAH   And you're a wife who has become a zoo-keeper.

            They walk up and down chatting to one another.

MRS NOAH   Noah, I felt something? Did you?

NOAH   The only thing I feel is my arm in yours ...

            The sons peep round and watch their parents.

SONS   Ahhh, look at the young lovers! Darby and Joan!

MRS NOAH   It felt like rain. If I hear or see a drop more rain, I'll scream!

SONS   Oh, no you won't!

            Mrs Noah is joined by the wives.

MRS NOAH   Oh, yes I will!

            They all start shouting again.

MRS NOAH   Will there be another flood? It's happened once, it could happen again.

NOAH   No more floods.

MRS NOAH   How do you know?

NOAH	God has promised.
MRS NOAH	But does God keep promises?
NOAH	Yes, God does! Which is more than you do!
MRS NOAH	Me?
NOAH	Yes, don't you remember what happened before the flood? You promised not to laugh if I told you what I was building. And when I told you about the ark – you laughed!
MRS NOAH	*(Joined by the other wives)* Oh, no I didn't!
NOAH	*(Joined by his sons)* Oh, yes you did!
	Children are invited to join in.
MRS NOAH	Well, maybe ... or maybe not. Anyway – it was funny. Whoever built a house-boat in the middle of the land?
HAM	A prophet.
SHEM	You mean an estate-agent looking for a quick profit?
HAM	Not that sort of profit, you twit.
MRS NOAH	Okay – I broke my promise. God may break the promise too, and flood the earth again ...
NOAH	God's different.
MRS NOAH	How?
NOAH	Well, God's greater than we are. When God says something will happen – it happens.
MRS NOAH	So when God says it won't flood again, that's an end to it – no more floods. How do you know?
NOAH	God gave me a sign that the promise would be kept. God has put the bow of war in the sky to show that the earth will never be destroyed again.
MRS NOAH	But where is this sign?
NOAH	Look! It's there – up above you, stretching like a bow from God to us! It's the rainbow!
MRS NOAH	*(Looking up)* A rainbow of promise. Whenever I see it, I shall remember today ... But rainbow or not, I'm getting wet! I'm going in. *(She turns to the children)* That's your lot!
	She rushes off to get an umbrella and returns with a sign that says Aahhh!
MRS NOAH	That really is your lot! *(She holds up the sign)*
ALL	Aahhh!

Story

You could use this story during **Exploring the Bible.** *It explains how the people of God understood the rainbow as a sign the God kept promises. It is an example of how the Bible story could be told. Remember that it is better to tell a story than read it.*

The ark was still; there was solid earth beneath it. The dove had not returned. This meant that she must have found a tree in which to nest! Noah realised that now they could all leave the ark. He waited until the door of the ark was opened and God told him to go out and start life again.

Noah, his wife, his sons, their wives and the animals all left the ark. Life began anew. Noah was thankful that God had spared him. It was a new beginning – just like new year with its new year resolutions and the possibility of a fresh start. Perhaps it was like this at the creation, Noah thought, when the earth was new and the world had just begun.

In the back of Noah's mind was a tiny fear which began to bother him. A flood had drowned the earth once – he had seen it! Could it happen again? Noah knew about making new year resolutions. They were promises. This year he had resolved he wouldn't kick the cat when he got angry. He kept his promise for the first day of the year – in fact, he kept it for a whole week – but then he forgot. The poor cat just had to keep out of his way! Noah knew he found keeping promises difficult. What about God? Did God keep promises? God had provided for Noah and his family and the animals. God had given them a second chance – but would there be a third chance and a fourth?

Somehow Noah knew that God was different from anyone else he had known. God was living – you could talk to God like a friend. Yet God was different from a human friend. Noah knew that he sometimes broke the promises he made to friends. God always kept promises. God had promised Noah that the earth would never again be flooded. God had said: 'As long as the world exists, there will be a time for planting and a time for harvest. There will always be cold and heat, summer and winter, day and night.' Noah knew that God would keep that promise.

As Noah was thinking and talking with God, there was a shower of rain. The sun was out. Perhaps, thought Noah, God is smiling! Then Noah saw a bright band of colours bridging the heavens to the earth, like a bow that is used to fire arrows. God had hung the bow of war in the sky to show that God was no longer angry with the world. When Noah saw it, he knew that God would always keep the promise. There would never be another flood.

Songs

The theme song: **The Rainbow Song** (see page 70)

'Abundantly' *Alleluya! No. 16*

'The earth is yours, O God' *Come and Praise No. 6*

'God made the earth' *Come and Praise No. 10*

'Song of Caedmon' *Come and Praise No. 13*

'Can you be sure that the rain will fall?' *Come and Praise No. 31*

'You shall go out with joy' *Come and Praise 2 No. 98*

Games

Give each child a pencil and a piece of paper with the colours of the rainbow written at the top. Give the children five minutes to list as many objects in the room as they can of the appropriate colours. (Younger participants could draw the objects.)

Creative resources

A woven picture (with a group)

You will need:

- 4 garden canes, about 40cm each in length,
- fine string, wool, grasses and leaves.

A simple loom can be made from four garden canes. Tie the canes together (see picture), attach thin string to one end of the cane, and wrap it around the canes as shown. Tie the end. Weave a collection of wool, grasses, leaves etc to represent the 'new creation.'

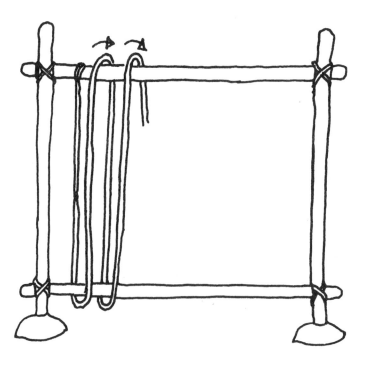

An individual loom

You will need:

- 2 sticks (green plant support sticks are ideal),
- wool.

Make a Mexican 'Eye of God' to put in your bedroom. It will remind you of the promise that God is always with you.

Tie the two sticks to form a cross. Wind wool around the cross, wrapping it around each arm five times before moving to the next (see illustration).

Use different rainbow colours, and finish by tying wool streamers to the arms and top.

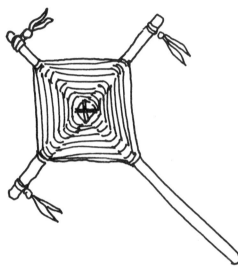

Rainbow wristband

Take threads in the seven rainbow colours and plait together into a single band. It needs to be long enough to go round a wrist and be tied. Cut a card disc about the size of a 50p piece and draw a personal design on it. Thread through the band (see illustration.)

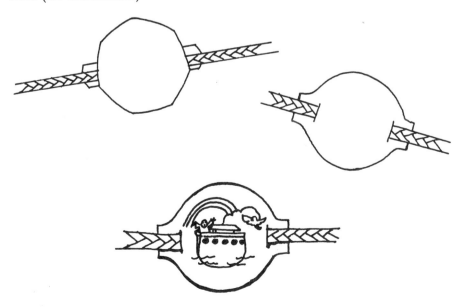

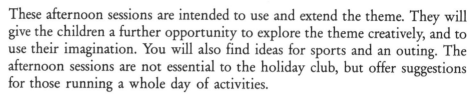

These afternoon sessions are intended to use and extend the theme. They will give the children a further opportunity to explore the theme creatively, and to use their imagination. You will also find ideas for sports and an outing. The afternoon sessions are not essential to the holiday club, but offer suggestions for those running a whole day of activities.

These sessions will depend on the resources and skills of the leaders in your particular situation. You may find that members of the congregation who are not otherwise involved in the holiday club are willing to come for an afternoon to share a skill with a small group of children. Parents may also respond if they are asked. The more choice of groups you can offer, the better.

The following ideas have worked well in other clubs:

1. Workshops

Music Workshop

If you have a group of musical children, the group could prepare and put on a short musical. It could be performed at the Celebration worship which concludes the week. Three possibilities are:

● *Captain Noah and his Floating Zoo* by Michael Flanders and J Horovitz (Novello).

● The Noah Jazz, music by Herbert Chappell, words by Tracie Lloyd (Clarabella Music Ltd in the series *All That Jazz).*

● *Noye's Fludde* by Benjamin Britten.

● *What a Good Idea!* (available from NCEC), includes a section on singing and making music.

Making Musical Instruments

Run a workshop on making simple musical instruments. Materials can be everyday objects such as rubber bands, yogurt pots and greaseproof paper. Below is a list of books to help you:

● *Making Musical Instruments* by Margaret Mclean (Macmillan 1982).

● *Musical Instruments Made To Be Played* by Ronald Roberts (Dyrad Press) – for the experts.

● *Sharing Sounds* David Evans (Longman) – how to develop musical skills.

● *Let's Make Music* by Alex Whinnom (Printforce) 6 Angel Hill Drive, Sutton, Surrey SM1 3BX.

Banner Making Workshop

Banners can be made cheaply and simply using scraps, or they can be more complex and expensive. You can choose for your situation. Some banners can be designed and made in an afternoon, so that the children have the pleasure of seeing their work completed. Material such as an old white sheet can be used for the backcloth. Draw bold designs on paper. Cut the pieces for the design, and any letters, from scraps of material that does not fray, such as felt. Stick your design on the backcloth with Copydex. Below is a list with plenty of ideas:

- *Banner Making to the King* by Priscilla Nunnerley.

- *An Army with Banners* by Priscilla Nunnerley.

- *Banners in His Name* Christian Banners, 9 Chestnut Court, Chestnut Lane, Amersham, Bucks HP6 6ED.

Cookery workshop

Children enjoy cooking together, but ensure you have plenty of space and sufficient helpers. It is essential that one of the adults has First Aid skills in case of burns and cuts. Make sure that there are sufficient copies of the recipe for each child to have one. Have all the ingredients ready before you begin cooking.

There will be books in your local library on children's cooking. If time is limited, recipes can be chosen that need little or no cooking – for example, crackolates, coconut ice or peppermint creams. Check the time factor in the recipe: it is important that children see the results of their activity at the end of the workshop.

Drama Workshop

The theme has scope for a range of activities from mime to impromtu drama. Here are some resources:

- *Lightning Sketches* by Paul Burbridge and Murray Watts of the Riding Lights Theatre Company (Hodder and Stoughton).

- *Move Yourselves* by Gordon and Ronni Lamont (Bible Society).

- *Using the Bible Series In Drama* By Steve and Janet Stickley with Jim Belben (Bible Society).

- *What a Good Idea!* (NCEC) includes sections on acting, mime and making puppets.

Painting

A group could make a *frieze* to tell the story. This could be an on-going activity, spaced over the week's sessions. Outline shapes to fill in can be created by laying a picture on an overhead projector. The picture is then projected on to a sheet of paper pinned to the wall. Move the projector until the picture is the size you require, then draw round the outline.

An alternative would be a painting of the new earth after the flood – or of a vision of the world as God intended.

Craft Workshop

The theme of *Rainbow People* is rich in craft possibilities. Various models of the animals can be made. *Papier mâché* can be used to cover a frame of chicken wire. Make some starch paste by mixing two tablespoons of plain or cornflour with a little cold water. Add half a litre of boiling water, stirring all the time. A teaspoon of soap powder will help prevent lumps, and a dash of antiseptic

slows down mould. Use the starch paste to build up layers of torn-up newspaper, or tissue towelling, over the chicken wire frame.

Animal models can be made from *play dough*. Mix in a saucepan: one cup of salt, two cups of plain flour and three teaspoons of cream of tartar. Gradually add two cups of water and two tablespoons of vegetable oil. Stir till smooth, then cook over a medium heat until stiff. Make several quantities of dough, and colour them differently using food colour or powder paint. If the dough is stored in an airtight container, it can be used over and over again.

Animal kites are fun to make and fly. Your kite could be in the shape of a butterfly, a bird or even a bat!

These books will give you some more ideas:

- *Animals to Make* (World Wild Life Fund Education Dept, WWF UK, Panda House, Weyside Park, Godalming, Surrey GU7 1XR).

- *Some Crafty Things to Do* by Karen Hale (Oxfam Education, Oxfam House, 274 Banbury Rd Oxford OX2 7DZ).

- *Fun with Kites* by John and Katie Dyson (Angus and Robertson).

- *What a Good Idea!* (available from NCEC) practical ideas and craft activities for children in the church. Includes sections on painting, modelling and producing audio-visuals.

2. Games

Outdoor games

These can vary from simple team games involving passing a ball or a bean bag, to a game of rounders or cricket. The activities need to be chosen with the participants ages and skill in mind – if children are not succeeding in a game, they quickly become bored. Try playing games which require *co-operation* – children enjoy learning to work together A wide selection of co-operative games can be found in:

- *Let's Co-operate* by Mildred Masheder (Peace Education Project, 6 Endsleigh St London WC1H 0DX).

Indoor games

Your choice of games will rely on the space available. Some indoor games can be quite active – 'Flap the Kipper', 'Dead Donkeys' and 'Squeak Piggy, Squeak' all have an animal theme! If space is limited, play board or card games such as 'Snakes and Ladders', a 'Beetle Drive' or 'Animal Snap'.

- *Over 300 Games for all Occasions* by Patrick Goodland (Scripture Union).

- *101 Games to Play* by Elizabeth Cooper (Treasure Press).

3. Sports Afternoon

Plan a whole afternoon of sports.
Divide the children into teams with a mixture of ages in each, and name each team after a different animal or bird. Let the teams compete in traditional events such as egg and spoon races, obstacle courses and three legged races. Try some of the cooperative games that are available. Any of these books will be helpful:

- *Let's play these Games* by Frances Lane (Printforce).

- *Let's Play these Games 2* by Frances Lane (Printforce).

- *Let's Co-operate* Mildred Masheder (Peace Education Project, 6 Endsleigh Street, London WC1H 0DX).

As a variation on a sports afternoon, or as an additional day, you could organize an animal *It's a Knock Out!* competition.

Mix the ages in each team and give each team an animal identity. Create games which reflect the theme. Have a simple scoring system such as timing each game – the team which successfully completes each game in the shortest time winning that event. The team which wins the most number of events will be the champions of the day!

Here are some examples of games:

- *Rescuing Mrs Noah:* Make a simple dummy (such as used for Guy Fawkes Night) for Mrs Noah. Create an obstacle course using old car tyres, ropes and large cardboard boxes. The team has to carry Mrs Noah over the obstacle course to rescue her from the flood.

- *Feed the Animals:* Make large animal faces with open mouths. The faces will need to have supports so that they can stand upright. Use bean bags or balls to 'feed' the animals.

- *Building the Ark:* Paint a large ark on corrogated cardboard. Create plenty of detail. Cut the cardboard into large jigsaw pieces. Pairs of children take turns to collect pieces of jigsaw from a pile and re-assemble them to 'build the ark'.

4. Outing

Choose an outing which reflects the theme. You could, for example, visit a safari park, or take part in a water-based activity: swimming, ice skating, a river trip or a visit to the seaside.

Make use of local resources; remember it is advisable not to make the journey too long.

5. Concert

Put on a concert for elderly people in your area. (Contact the local day-centre, club, or old-peoples' home well in advance to arrange a date.) The children could share some of the *Rainbow People* drama and songs. Let the music workshop perform! The cookery workshop could provide a simple tea.

THE RAINBOW SONG

God The Artist

by Dr Dr June Boyce-Tillman

♩. = 84

D · **Em** · **Bm** · **A**
I want to make___ a rain - bow And paint it with my

D · **G** · **D**
love,_____ But first I'll make___ the paint - box, Link

Em · **A** · **D** · **G**
earth with heaven a - bove._____ I'll start off with the

D · **Bm** · **F#** · **Bm**
dark end And move to - wards___ the bright,_____ Then

Em · **Bm** · **G** · **D**
blend them all___ to - ge - ther To make a light that's white.___

Chorus **D** · **D** · **D** · **D**
We're ri - ding on a rain - bow, We're ri - ding on a rain - bow, We're

D · **D** · **A** · **D**
ri - ding on a rain - bow That tells us of God's love!_____

1. I want to make a rainbow
   And paint it with my love,
   But first I'll make the paintbox,
   Link earth with heaven above.
   I'll start off with the dark end
   And move towards the bright,
   Then blend them altogether
   To make a light that's white.

   Chorus   We're riding on a rainbow,
            We're moving on a rainbow,
            That tells us of God's love!

2. So first I'll make the violet
   By touching purple shoots,
   The indigo will take longer
   I'll need some deep, dark roots.
   The green will not be too hard
   Just wait till spring begins,
   For blue I'll need some water
   And flashy fishy fins. *Chorus*

3. The yellow lies on the seashore
   And glows in summer sun,
   The oranges have ripened
   Now autumn has begun.
   The red I'll find in winter
   In berries on the tree,
   Now all my paints are ready
   A miracle you'll see. *Chorus*

4. For there's another canvas
   That isn't in the sky,
   A space in every person,
   A heart where tears can cry,
   A place where joy can spring up
   Like sunshine after rain,
   A gentle creamy paper
   Where I can paint again. *Chorus*

5. I'll use the same old colours
   With which I paint the sky,
   Remind them of the promise
   I made in years gone by.
   Recall in them my loving,
   My caring for my world,
   Each time they see the rainbow
   Across the earth unfurled. *Chorus*

The chorus could be turned into a song in its own right for younger children. Extra verses could be added – for example:

We're sliding down a rainbow...
We're jumping over a rainbow...
We're skipping along a rainbow...

Actions could be added.

As adults we have come to love the Bible. We have discovered how its stories speak to, reflect, and throw light on our own experiences of life. Through its accounts of the revelation of God – particularly in Jesus – the Bible brings meaning to our lives. It draws us to commitment in a relationship with God within a community of faith – the church. Naturally, we desire this experience for our children, and want them to relate the Bible story to their present experience.

Sometimes, when we look at certain sections of the Bible, we realise the complexity of the task of introducing it to children. The story of the flood is a good example of this. We think we know the story, but if we take another look we realise that it has hidden depths. These should be plumbed before the story is shared.

The account of the flood story is a long one and is worth reading straight through. *(Genesis 6.11-9.17)* It is a good idea to do this as an exercise, and to jot down any questions that occur to you as you read it.

In a careful reading of the text, discrepancies may begin to appear – for example: the number of pairs of animals entering the ark. At one point we are told there was a pair of each animal *(Genesis 6.19);* later there appear to be seven pairs of clean and two of unclean animals *(7.2).* The flood lasts for forty days *(7.17);* and for a hundred and fifty days *(7.24).* The name of God varies. (In Hebrew two names are used – *Jahweh* and *Elohim;* in most translations we find 'Lord' *(7.1)* and 'God' *6.12).* Scholars account for this by reminding us that in most cultures there is a 'flood story'. It is likely that in *Genesis* we have two, or even three, traditions interwoven. To answer questions about the origin of the traditions it is useful to look at a story from Babylon.

From Babylon comes the *Epic of Gilgamesh,* dating from about 1800 BC. The epic tells of a man who is warned about a coming disaster, builds a boat, takes his family and representatives of the animals on board with him, and is saved from a flood which covers the mountain tops. The Jews may have heard this story as exiles in Babylon. The fact that there are parallels between *Genesis* and the *Epic of Gilgamesh* suggest to scholars that the two stories are connected and may come from a single, older source.

Stories of flooding by rain occur among many different peoples, including the Australian Aborigines, the Innuit (Eskimos), and the American Indians. Accounts are told in countries as diverse as India and Greece. It is unlikely that these communities had any communications with one another – and yet they all have a common tradition of a flood story. It may be that the concepts underlying a flood tradition lie deep within the human psyche. One of the questions asked about the flood story concerns historicity. An expedition recently set out to find Mount Ararat and the remains of the ark, believing that the biblical story described an actual event. Nothing was found. However, in the area of the Tigris-Euphrates Valley, archaeologists have discovered levels of what are called 'clean water-laid clay'. These layers suggest that on several occasions there was local flooding which destroyed whole communities. One particular layer was eight feet deep. At the time it would seem to have covered the entire world. This layer was especially evident at the excavation of Ur of the Chaldees, the city from which Abraham came *(Genesis 11.31).*

For the writer of *Genesis,* the 'hero' of the story is God; the author is not concerned about whether or not there was a historical flood. The key to his story is its meaning. The biblical story has a universal truth to tell, and is as significant today as when it was first told. Some people would use the word *myth* to describe the story – the word 'myth' simply means 'a story with meaning'.

At one level it is easy to use this story with children because of the appeal of the animals and the possibilities for creative work, although we can be in danger of emasculating the story if we omit its more difficult concepts – those, for example, which concern destruction. The early church father Gregory the Great, however, said that scripture 'provides water in which lambs may walk and elephants may swim'. How, then, can we be true to the meaning of the story and yet provide 'shallow water' for the children, where they can immediately become involved both emotionally and imaginatively, and yet are enabled to return in later years to explore the story in greater depth?

The flood story is about deep experiences such as being overwhelmed by evil and its consequences, through which God's saving grace is known. These experiences are also true for children. They are often aware of the frightening power of their own emotions of anger and jealousy; they know their need for safe places; they need the constancy of promises kept and the assurance that despite their unkind actions they are loved, can receive forgiveness and can begin anew.

In recent years a book was published with the title *The Bible – a Child's Playground* (R & G Gobbel, SCM Press 1986). Its authors advocate the central task of using the Bible with children as that of 'engagement', and encourage children to play with ideas from the Bible. Thus the children may bring two sets of stories together – their own and the text. In this lively encounter – as children explore, think, feel, wonder and question – they see the revelation of God in the Bible as speaking to them.

Pages 74–88 may be photocopied, and need not be declared in any return in respect of any photocopy licence.

Holiday Club Questionnaire

Please complete and return by .... the first day of the Holiday club.

Child's name ....

Child's Address ....

....

.... Telephone ....

Medical Matters

Name of Doctor .... Telephone: ....

Has your child any medical condition that we should know about? **Yes/No**

If Yes, please give details...

....

....

....

If your child will be bringing any medicines or tablets please let us know.

Going home

Will your child be:

a. Allowed to return home unaccompanied **Yes/No**

b. Collected by an adult **Yes/No**

If the adult is not a parent, please state who will have authority to collect your child:

....

Contact number

Please give a name and telephone number to contact in case of emergency.

Name: .... Telephone:.....................

Thank you for your assistance in completing this form.

Signature .... Date ....

Dear Parent,

Holiday Club . . . . **at**. . . . .

Long summer holiday? Wondering what to do with the children?

. . . .
invites local children aged 5 to 12 years inclusive to join in the fun of a holiday club.

What happens?

Children come together in age groups for a Christian based programme of learning, creative activities and lots of fun and games.

When is it?

From . . . .   to . . . .

from .am   to . . . . .pm

Please bring a packed lunch.

Where is it?

It is based at . . . .

Supervision

It will be supervised at all times by experienced volunteers.

What is the cost?

A registration fee of £ . . . . per child for the week is requested to offset the considerable expense involved in running a scheme of this kind.

How do I apply?

Please complete the tear off slip and return in a sealed envelope marked HC to:

. . . .
. . . .

— —

Reply

Please reserve . . . . place(s) for the following children:

. . . .   DOB. . . . .

. . . .   DOB. . . . .

. . . .   DOB. . . . .

Name   . . . .   Telephone:

Address: . . . .   Home . . . .

              . . . .   Work . . . .

I enclose £. . . . . (cash or cheque payable to . . . .) to cover the cost of registration.

Spot the Difference

How many differences can *you* spot? (There are 10!)

Noah's Ark

Read these instructions before cutting!

Hull and Deck (shape one, on opposite page.)
Colour or paint, and then cut out the shape round the heavy black line. Fold the sides of the deck downwards, as indicated by the arrows. Fold tabs A and B inwards.

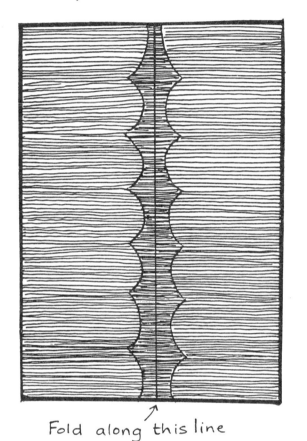

Fold along this line

Fold tabs C inward and glue to the underside of the deck. Put a small drop of glue near X (the ends of the hull) and stick the sides together at each end.

Spread glue on tab A as indicated, and attach it to the underside of tab B. This makes a flat base so that your ark will stand up.

Cabin (shape two, bottom of page.)
Colour and cut round the heavy black lines. Fold sides and end of cabin upwards from the base. Fold tabs D inwards, and tabs E outwards. Stick tabs D to the end of the cabin.

Roof (shape three, left.)
Colour and cut out, fold in half as indicated. Take your cabin and spread a little glue onto the back of tabs E. Lower the roof onto the tabs, and press into place.

Finishing the Ark
Take the hull and deck and spread a little glue on the central clear area. Stick the cabin into position on the deck. (This is easier if you press gently with your finger from underneath.)

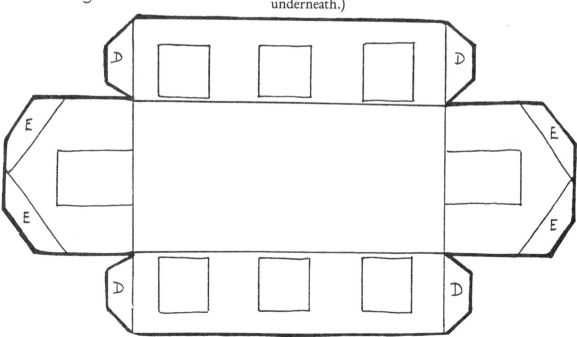

Hull and Deck.

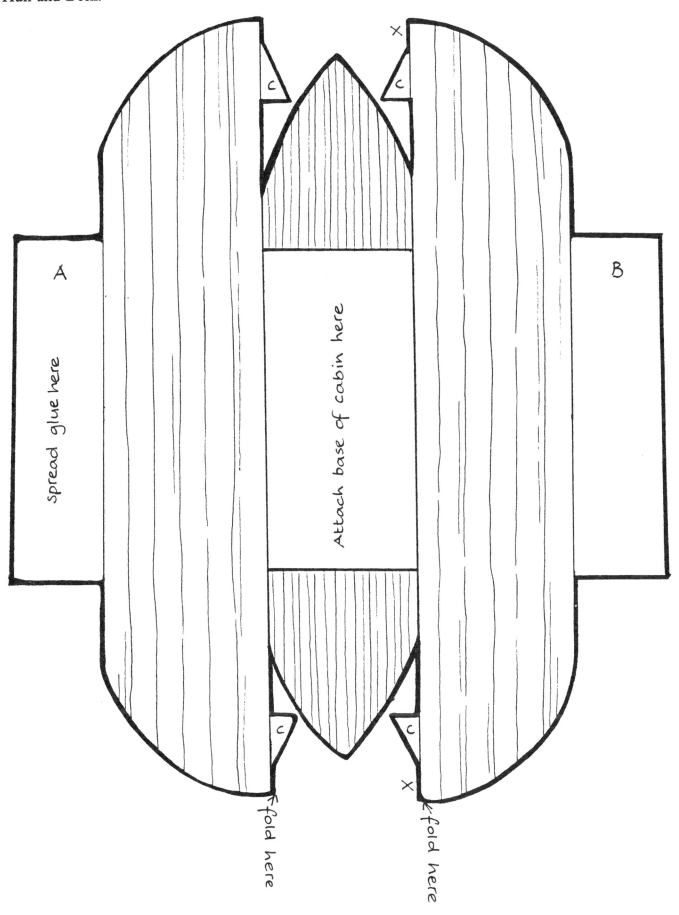

People and Animals

The following pages contain templates of people and animals which can be photocopied and used in a variety of ways.

Attached to card, they can be made to stand up (see diagrams). They can then be arranged around the model ark to form a 'Rainbow Scene'.

Noah mobile

Stick card to backs of figures to make them stand

Stick to card and add a lolly stick for a Noah puppet

slit

fold

fold

Cut out in double thickness card.

Fold in half to make figure stand up.

A Noah Puppet

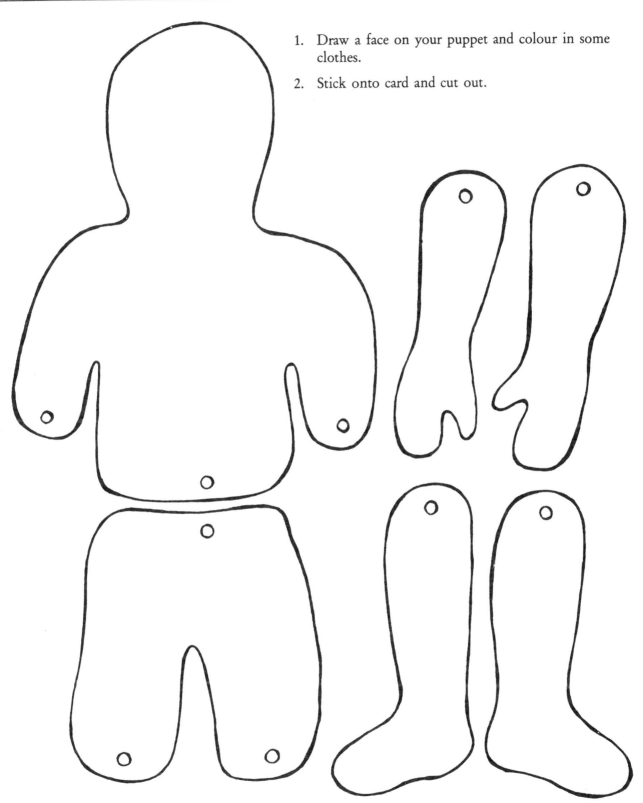

1. Draw a face on your puppet and colour in some clothes.

2. Stick onto card and cut out.

3. Fasten through marked holes with paper fasteners. (Not too tight.)

4. Slip a piece of string under the arms and behind the head. Your puppet will now dance!

A Rainbow to Colour

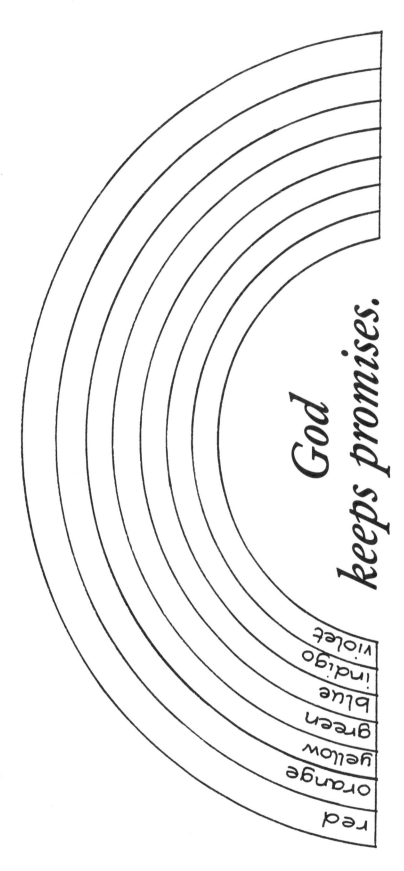

God keeps promises.

*While the earth remains,
seedtime and harvest
day and night
summer and winter
will not cease.*

red
orange
yellow
green
blue
indigo
violet

Word Search 1

```
E L E P H A N T M
M I H Z E B R A O
D O V E Q A E O N
R N O C A T C U K
A A R U S N A K E
B E A R H R M A Y
B G V S E S E I L
I E E H E N L E L
T E N W P S B E E
```

BAT	DOVE	RABBIT
BEAR	ELEPHANT	RAVEN
BEE	HEN	SHEEP
CAT	LION	SNAKE
CAMEL	MONKEY	ZEBRA

Word Search 2

```
B E A R M O C L I O N K U
A U R A V E N A H Y R A X
T S T U R T L E M E E N H
O H R T D O V E O E N G R
G P E L E P H A N T L A H
O I E D Z R S E K S Q R I
R S R L G E F U E N R O N
I N C A I E B L Y A A O O
L A S A F C H R Y K B A C
L I I H T F A O A E B E E
A L L E E P E N G U I N R
A C O C K E R E L G T L O
E H I P P O P O T A M U S
```

BAT	GIRAFFE	PENGUIN
BEAR	GORILLA	RABBIT
BEE	HEDGEHOG	RAVEN
BUTTERFLY	HEN	RHINOCEROS
CAMEL	HIPPOPOTAMUS	SHEEP
CAT	HYRAX	SNAIL
COCKEREL	KANGAROO	SNAKE
DOVE	LION	TURTLE
ELEPHANT	MONKEY	ZEBRA
	PELICAN	

The animals listed are all to be found in this grid in one of the following ways:

By reading along the lines from left to right.

By reading down a column.

By reading diagonally down from left to right.

All these animals are either mentioned or illustrated in this book. When an animal has been found put a line through the letters or draw a ring around them. When all the animals are found there will be some unused letters. Copy them down from left to right. These should spell the names of four other creatures that are mentioned in the Bible.

SOLUTION: WORD SEARCH 1

SOLUTION: WORD SEARCH 2

MOUSE
HORSE
QUAIL
EAGLE

Which Animal?

Shem, Ham and Japhet are helping their father by leading some of the animals into the ark. Can you discover which animal each son is leading?

Shem _____   Ham _____   Japheth _____

Butterfly and Snake

Colour the snake in bright colours and cut it out carefully along the heavy black lines.

Tie a knot in a length of strong cotton and thread it through the snake's head.

Hang up your snake like this:

Try making a butterfly at rest

This crawling snake is easy to cut out and make. You could decorate it with sequins and silver paper, or paint it brightly on both sides.

Colour the butterfly and decorate it brightly.

Cut it out and fold along the dotted line, then hang it up like this:

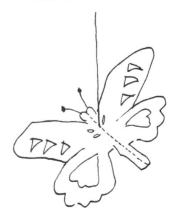